THE
1,500-Calorie-a-Day Cookbook

NANCY S. HUGHES

Mc Graw Hill

New York Chicago San Francisco Lisbon London Madrid Mexico City
Milan New Delhi San Juan Seoul Singapore Sydney Toronto

The **McGraw·Hill** Companies

Library of Congress Cataloging-in-Publication Data

Hughes, Nancy S.
   The 1500-calorie-a-day cookbook / Nancy S. Hughes.
       p.   cm.
   ISBN-13: 978-0-07-154385-9
   ISBN-10: 0-07-154385-6
   1. Reducing diets—Recipes.   I. Title.   II. Title: The fifteen hundred
calorie-a-day cookbook.

   RM222.2.H848   2009
   641.5′635—dc22   2008034454

1 2 3 4 5 6 7 8 9 10 11 12 13 14 15 16 17 18 19   FGR/FGR   0 9 8

ISBN 978-0-07-154385-9
MHID   0-07-154385-6

Interior design by Think Design Group LLC

McGraw-Hill books are available at special quantity discounts to use as premiums and sales promotions or for use in corporate training programs. To contact a representative, please visit the Contact Us pages at www.mhprofessional.com.

This book is printed on acid-free paper.

To my husband, Greg, who understands the real me, pulls me in when I get carried away, puts things into perspective, and then helps me fly—to get carried away again, but with direction.

And to my children,

Will and Kelly and now Miss Molly Catherine, who pop in for random tastings, total chaos, and tons of opinions—welcomed opinions.

Annie, who finds the pure joy in good food and the "coziness" of a good conversation—over that good food.

Taft, who still patiently comes by to "unblink" the flashing clock and other such technology adjustments I don't have time—nor bother—to deal with.

You've all found the deep passion that steers your heart in each of your lives and in each of your professions—what true accomplishments. (Of course, I take sole credit for showing you the way.) I love you!

Contents

Acknowledgments

To Monica Davis, Robin Brinker, Liz Dixon, and Melanie Crane for all the long hours helping to "get it just right"; having mind-swirling conversations; and caring so much for the sake of the book, the sake of the recipe, and the sake of not having to test it one more time!

To Judy Wilcox, for letting me pick her "nutritionally genius" brain and helping me make simple sense out of it all!

To my editor, Sarah Pelz, for having a great thought, digging deep and popping up with an even greater idea, and working with me to make this book happen. Thanks, Sarah, for your collected, calm personality to match my collected but over-the-top, excitable personality. Teamwork at its best!

Thanks for helping to bring it together!

Introduction

Our schedules are so crazy, and eating healthy is not always at the top of the priority list. We tend to let the healthy aspect slide a little, along with our quality of food. So our good intentions tend to slip through the cracks, along with our health. It can get away from us one bite at a time. By the same token, we can improve our quality of health one bite at a time!

With this book, it's actually enjoyable to stick to a healthy, low-calorie meal plan. Just because you're trying to lose weight or watch your calorie intake, it doesn't mean you have to sacrifice flavor, taste, variety, or the simple pleasures food can bring. Remember "snack time" growing up? It not only helped refuel us between meals but also was fun! But what we didn't realize was that it was also portion controlled—a couple of graham crackers and milk, an apple, or a handful of nuts, for example. And so it is with this book: grab a fast-fix snack in the middle of the morning and then again in the afternoon, just like you used to do. It's a fun and easy way to stay on track, as is the entire book.

How to Use This Book

The recipes in this book are designed to make it easy for you to eat healthy, satisfying food all day long and keep to 1,500 calories a day—without having to count calories or prepare complicated meals. In these pages, you'll find 150 recipes for filling breakfasts; stick-to-the-ribs lunches and dinners; tasty snacks; and delicious, guilt-free desserts. Every day you get to choose three meals, two snacks, and one dessert. Breakfast, plus one snack, plus lunch, plus another snack, plus dinner, plus dessert—all for just 1,500 calories!

All breakfasts, lunches, and dinners are approximately 350 calories each. All snacks and desserts are approximately 150 calories each. So no matter what combination you choose from the various chapters, you'll come up with about 1,500 calories a day. If you cut out the dessert, it can be a 1,350-calorie day, but who wants to give up dessert? There's no need. This is not a diet plan, but rather a delicious way to take you through the day in a healthy way.

This book contains a month's worth of breakfasts, snacks and appetizers, lunches, dinners, and desserts that are calorie controlled to help you stay within weight-loss parameters while getting tons of flavor and nutritional benefits. And they're fast, really fast. Each recipe takes 30 minutes or less to make—and that's not just for one part of the meal, but for the entire meal. There's one main recipe for each meal and purposely simple sides to go along with it.

As in all of my books, all of the recipes are family-friendly but will also satisfy the savvy eaters in your life. You can find all of the ingredients in traditional supermarkets, so no extra grocery runs to specialty food shops are necessary. The ingredient lists are short

to keep the shopping, prep, and cleanup time to a minimum. Using high-flavor ingredients, a variety of easy cooking techniques, and multi-ingredient items such as seasoning blends or salsa are just some of the secrets to these great-tasting quick-fixers.

An added bonus is that these recipes are interchangeable! Desserts can be snacks, snacks can be desserts, breakfasts can be lunches, lunches can be dinners. Many dinners can be frozen for other meals down the road or brown-bagged for lunches the next day. It all depends on your mood.

Throughout the Book, You'll Get

▶ **Recipe and accompaniments:** There's one written recipe for the main course in each meal and a list of recommended side dishes.

▶ **Streamlined ingredient list:** The lists of ingredients are purposefully kept short for ease in shopping, storing, prepping, and cleaning up. But while the recipes are short on ingredients, they're not short on flavor! If you're counting, they each have from six to eight ingredients, not counting salt, pepper, water, and optionals.

▶ **Time-Shaver Tips and Cook's Notes:** I've included helpful sidebars with quick info, such as healthy tips, shortcuts, and quick, general information to keep you "in the know."

▶ **Total yield and serving sizes:** To make it easier to know how much the recipe will make, I've provided both total yields and serving sizes. The majority of the recipes are designed to serve four, but most can easily be broken down to serve two or even one.

▶ **Nutritional analysis:** A full nutritional analysis is included per serving for the entire meal and for each component of the meal. (Meal-inclusive nutrition information follows the recipe title; many snacks and the desserts have only individual nutritional information because they do not include accompaniments.) This makes for easy side-swapping, so if you aren't in the mood for one accompaniment, you can easily change it for one you do want, while still being mindful of the calorie count.

These nutritional values were calculated by ESHA Research software or provided by food manufacturers in decimals, which were then rounded out to the nearest whole number. Calculations for an entire meal may appear to vary slightly from the nutritional analysis for individual meal components, but they are accurate based on these exact decimal values.

▶ **Nutritional benefits:** This feature is my personal favorite. These notes inform you when you're getting an extra boost of fiber, vitamin A, vitamin C, calcium, or iron.

Rating Good and Excellent Sources

In my recipes, whenever a meal contains a good or an excellent source of any of the fol-lowing nutritional benefits, it reads, "Good source of . . ." or "Excellent source of . . ."; this will help you stay better informed of what you are actually eating while you're enjoying it. These nutritional values are calculated for the *entire* meal (main recipe plus side dishes).

The Food and Drug Administration (FDA) has established criteria to help us understand the nutritional benefits and claims of what is a "good" or an "excellent" source of certain vitamins and minerals. The following is a simplified explanation of the whys and wherefores of it all.

To be a good source of vitamin A, vitamin C, calcium, or iron, a serving has to provide at least 10 percent of the recommended daily allowance (RDA), and an excellent source has to provide 20 percent of the RDA.

To be a good source of fiber, a serving has to provide no less than 2.5 to 4.9 grams, and an excellent source yields 5 grams or more per serving.

Vitamin A

▶ **Why is it important?** It keeps eyes and skin healthy and helps to protect against infections.

▶ **What foods provide it?** The best sources are dark green leafy vegetables and orange fruits and vegetables. Choose from all fresh, frozen, canned, or dried vegetables and fruits.

▶ **What should I look for on the nutrition label?** A serving providing at least 10 percent of the RDA is considered a good source of vitamin A; one providing at least 20 percent is considered an excellent source.

Vitamin C

▶ **Why is it important?** It helps heal cuts and wounds; keeps teeth and gums healthy; helps promote a healthy immune system; and aids in iron absorption.

▶ **What foods provide it?** Choose from fresh, frozen, canned, or dried vegetables and fruits.

▶ **What should I look for on the nutrition label?** A serving providing at least 10 percent of the RDA is considered a good source of vitamin C; one providing at least 20 percent is considered an excellent source.

Iron

▶ **Why is it important?** Iron is a mineral that is essential for carrying oxygen through the blood.

▶ **What foods provide it?** Among the foods that are relatively high in iron are lean red meat, pork, poultry, fish, soybeans, spinach, beans, and eggs.

▶ **What should I look for on the nutritional label?** A serving providing at least 10 percent of the RDA is considered a good source of iron; one providing at least 20 percent is considered an excellent source.

Fiber

▶ **Why is it important?** Fiber is important for the health of the digestive system and for lowering cholesterol. It helps give a feeling of fullness with fewer calories.

▶ **What foods provide it?** Among the foods that are relatively high in fiber are plant-based foods such as fruit, vegetables, whole grains, beans, and cereal products.

▶ **What should I look for on the nutritional label?** A serving providing at least 2.5 to 4.9 grams is considered a good source of fiber; one providing at least 5 grams is considered an excellent source.

Calcium

▶ **Why is it important?** Calcium is necessary for building bones and teeth and for maintaining bone mass, possibly reducing the risk of osteoporosis.

▶ **What foods provide it?** Dairy products are the primary sources. Other, nondairy sources are fortified cereals, calcium-fortified soy beverage, salmon, and dark green leafy vegetables such as spinach and broccoli.

▶ **What should I look for on the nutritional label?** A serving providing at least 10 percent of the RDA is considered a good source of calcium; one providing at least 20 percent is considered an excellent source.

Free Seasonings

The following seasoning suggestions can add tons of flavor to your dishes—whether entrees, salads, or side dishes—without adding tons of fat!

Keep these spice blends on hand:

Creole
Mexican
Greek
Lemon pepper
Italian
Thai
Southwestern
Mesquite
Moroccan

Use fresh ingredients like these to pick up the flavors of other ingredients:

Fresh lemon, lime, and orange juice and grated rind
Grated gingerroot
Finely chopped green onion
Finely chopped jalapeño
Fresh garlic (put through a garlic press for the best flavor)
Fresh herbs

Note: If you're adding these ingredients to recipes that are being cooked, add them at the very end of the cooking time for peak flavor.

Other products you can use to season salads, veggies, and entrees include the following:

Salad spritzers
Hot pepper sauces (There's a wide variety on the market.)
Salsas and spaghetti sauce
Butter pump sprays (Be sure to count your pumps—they add up!)
Butter granules
Fat-free sour cream
Fat-free salad dressings
A small amount of light soy sauce

A Final Suggestion

Although the recipe ingredients are given in volume measurements for the most part, it would be helpful to purchase a small food scale—it's inexpensive and indispensable! It can save you from guesswork about ingredient amounts (especially with meats, poultry, and seafood) and easily keeps you on track.

1

Breakfasts

POULTRY- AND MEAT-BASED

► Hearty Breakfast Pork Chops au Jus

► Ham and Asparagus with Lemony Cream Sauce

► Canadian Bacon Stackers

► Simply Sizzling Steak and Onions

► Sausage and Glazed Pineapple

► Creamy Swiss and Ham Mini Bagels

EGG-BASED

► Broccoli-Bacon Frittata

► Knife-and-Fork Breakfast Tortillas

► Country Garden Frittata

► Mini Ham and Potato Quiches

► English Muffin Pizza Scramble

► Bacon and Egg Breakfast Sandwich

► Fried Eggs on Rice and Black Beans

BREADS, PANCAKES, AND GRAIN-BASED

► Drop Biscuits and Creamy Apricot Spread

► Rustic Breakfast Roll-Ups

► Baguette Cheese Toast

► Cinnamon French Toast with Cheesecake Sauce

► Light "Italian" Toast with Fresh Citrus Sauce

► Peach-Cranberry Pancakes

► Mushroom and Red Pepper Cheese-Smothered Grits

► Apple-Honey Oatmeal

► Fresh Berry Oatmeal with Sweet Cream

► On-the-Run Breakfast Cookies

FRUIT- AND VEGETABLE-BASED

► Hash Brown Casserole

► Broiled Breakfast Tomatoes

► Apple Halvers

► Big-Bowl Cereal Parfait

► Tropical Fruit and Yogurt Platters

► Peach-Pineapple Breakfast Drink

► Travel Mug Breakfast

1

Hearty Breakfast Pork Chops au Jus

with Creamy Grits, Wheat Toast, and Fresh Orange Slices

Calories 350; total fat 6g (saturated fat 2g); protein 30g; carbohydrates 44g; fiber 7g; cholesterol 70mg; sodium 500mg; vitamin A 6%; vitamin C 120%; calcium 10%; iron 15%

4 boneless pork chops, trimmed of fat (1 pound total)

¼ teaspoon garlic powder

¼ teaspoon black pepper

⅓ cup water

½ teaspoon Worcestershire sauce

½ teaspoon instant coffee granules

¼ teaspoon salt

▶ Sprinkle both sides of the pork chops with the garlic powder and black pepper. Heat a medium nonstick skillet over medium-high heat until hot, and coat the skillet with cooking spray. Cook the pork chops 4 minutes on each side or until barely pink in the center.

▶ Meanwhile, combine the remaining ingredients in a small bowl and set aside.

▶ Place the pork chops on a plate. Add the Worcestershire mixture to the skillet and bring to a boil; boil 1 to 1½ minutes or until reduced to 2 tablespoons. Drizzle evenly over the pork chops.

Calories 160; total fat 6g (saturated fat 2g); protein 25g; carbohydrates 1g; fiber 0g; cholesterol 70mg; sodium 230mg; vitamin A 0%; vitamin C 2%; calcium 2%; iron 6%

COOK'S NOTE: *This is a very intense topping; a small amount goes a long way.*

Excellent source of fiber and vitamin C

Good source of calcium and iron

Makes 4 pork chops total

Serves 4 *(3 ounces cooked pork, ½ cup cooked grits, 1 slice toast, 1 teaspoon fruit spread, and 1 orange per serving)*

SERVE WITH

2 cups cooked grits seasoned with ¼ teaspoon each salt and pepper

Calories 70; total fat 0g (saturated fat 0g); protein 2g; carbohydrates 16g; fiber 0g; cholesterol 0mg; sodium 150mg; vitamin A 0%; vitamin C 0%; calcium 0%; iron 4%

4 slices reduced-calorie whole-wheat bread, toasted, and 4 teaspoons fruit spread

Calories 50; total fat 0g (saturated fat 0g); protein 2g; carbohydrates 12g; fiber 4g; cholesterol 0mg; sodium 120mg; vitamin A 0%; vitamin C 0%; calcium 2%; iron 4%

4 medium oranges, sliced

Calories 60; total fat 0g (saturated fat 0g); protein 1g; carbohydrates 15g; fiber 3g; cholesterol 0mg; sodium 0mg; vitamin A 6%; vitamin C 120%; calcium 6%; iron 0%

Ham and Asparagus with Lemony Cream Sauce

with Raspberry-Cranberry Juice, Pink Grapefruit Sections, and Wheat Toast

Calories 350; total fat 11g (saturated fat 3g); protein 21g; carbohydrates 47g; fiber 8g; cholesterol 245mg; sodium 800mg; vitamin A 60%; vitamin C 120%; calcium 15%; iron 30%

1 cup water

1 pound asparagus (about 20 spears), trimmed

1¼ cups (6 ounces) extra-lean turkey ham, sliced thin and chopped

¾ cup nonfat plain yogurt

2 tablespoons plus 2 teaspoons diet mayonnaise

2 teaspoons prepared mustard

4 large hard-boiled eggs, peeled and chopped

▶ Bring water to boil in a large skillet over medium-high heat; add the asparagus, return to a boil, cover, and cook 2 minutes or until just tender crisp. Drain well and place on a serving platter. Cover to keep warm.

▶ Dry the skillet with a paper towel and place over medium heat; coat the skillet with cooking spray. Add the turkey ham and cook 1 minute, stirring frequently; set aside on a separate plate.

▶ Reduce the heat to medium low; add the yogurt, mayonnaise, and mustard and cook 30 seconds, stirring constantly. Do not bring to a boil. Spoon evenly over the asparagus and top with the ham and chopped egg.

Calories 200; total fat 11g (saturated fat 3g); protein 18g; carbohydrates 10g; fiber 3g; cholesterol 245mg; sodium 680mg; vitamin A 25%; vitamin C 15%; calcium 10%; iron 25%

> 🥄 **COOK'S NOTE:** *This makes a great entree as well. Serve with whole-wheat dinner rolls instead of the toast.*

Excellent source of fiber, vitamins A and C, and iron

Good source of calcium

Makes about 20 asparagus spears, 1 cup ham, and 1 cup sauce total

Serves 4 *(about 5 asparagus spears, ¼ cup ham, ¼ cup sauce, ½ cup juice, ¾ cup grapefruit, and 1 slice toast per serving)*

SERVE WITH

2 cups raspberry-cranberry juice

> Calories 50; total fat 0g (saturated fat 0g); protein 0g; carbohydrates 13g; fiber 0g; cholesterol 0mg; sodium 0mg; vitamin A 0%; vitamin C 10%; calcium 0%; iron 2%

3 cups pink grapefruit sections

> Calories 60; total fat 0g (saturated fat 0g); protein 1g; carbohydrates 14g; fiber 2g; cholesterol 0mg; sodium 0mg; vitamin A 30%; vitamin C 100%; calcium 2%; iron 0%

4 slices reduced-calorie whole-wheat bread, toasted

> Calories 40; total fat 0g (saturated fat 0g); protein 2g; carbohydrates 9g; fiber 4g; cholesterol 0mg; sodium 120mg; vitamin A 0%; vitamin C 0%; calcium 2%; iron 4%

3

Canadian Bacon Stackers

with Bran Muffins, Cantaloupe Wedges, and Cold Milk

Calories 350; total fat 8g (saturated fat 3g); protein 21g; carbohydrates 50g; fiber 6g; cholesterol 25mg; sodium 890mg; vitamin A 70%; vitamin C 100%; calcium 35%; iron 15%

1 medium poblano chili pepper, seeded and chopped fine (¾ cup)

4 slices Canadian bacon (4 ounces total)

1 large tomato, cut into 4 slices

½ cup (2 ounces) shredded reduced-fat sharp cheddar cheese

▶ Heat a medium nonstick skillet over medium-high heat until hot, and coat the skillet with cooking spray. Add the pepper and coat with cooking spray; cook 2 minutes or until beginning to brown on the edges, stirring frequently. Remove from the skillet and set aside on a separate plate.

▶ Recoat the skillet with cooking spray. Add the Canadian bacon and cook 1 minute; turn. Reduce heat to medium low; top with the tomato slices, cheese, and pepper; cover and cook 5 minutes or until cheese melts. Remove from heat, uncover, and let stand 3 minutes to absorb flavors and cool slightly.

Calories 110; total fat 5g (saturated fat 2.5g); protein 10g; carbohydrates 5g; fiber 1g; cholesterol 25mg; sodium 520mg; vitamin A 15%; vitamin C 50%; calcium 10%; iron 2%

TIME-SHAVER TIP: If poblanos are not available, use ½ medium green bell pepper and a dash of cayenne pepper.

COOK'S NOTE: Throughout this book, ingredients are sometimes coated with cooking spray while cooking. This helps them cook more evenly and prevents drying them out or scorching them, without adding more fat.

Excellent source of fiber, vitamins A and C, and calcium

Good source of iron

Makes 4 stacks total

Serves 4 *(1 stack, 1 muffin, 1 cantaloupe wedge, and ¾ cup milk per serving)*

SERVE WITH

4 bran muffins with raisins

Calories 150; total fat 2.5g (saturated fat 0g); protein 4g; carbohydrates 30g; fiber 4g; cholesterol 0mg; sodium 260mg; vitamin A 0%; vitamin C 2%; calcium 4%; iron 10%

½ medium cantaloupe, seeded and cut into 4 wedges

Calories 25; total fat 0g (saturated fat 0g); protein 1g; carbohydrates 6g; fiber 1g; cholesterol 0mg; sodium 10mg; vitamin A 45%; vitamin C 40%; calcium 0%; iron 0%

3 cups fat-free milk

Calories 70; total fat 0g (saturated fat 0g); protein 7g; carbohydrates 10g; fiber 0g; cholesterol 0mg; sodium 100mg; vitamin A 8%; vitamin C 2%; calcium 20%; iron 0%

S'imply S'izzling Steak and Onions

with Hash Browns and Honeydew Melon

Calories 350; total fat 8g (saturated fat 2g); protein 30g; carbohydrates 41g; fiber 5g; cholesterol 50mg; sodium 420mg; vitamin A 80%; vitamin C 80%; calcium 4%; iron 10%

1 medium onion, sliced thin (1 cup)

1 pound boneless top round steak, about ½ inch thick, trimmed of fat and cut into 4 pieces

1 teaspoon salt-free steak seasoning grill blend

¼ cup water

¼ teaspoon salt

▶ Place a large nonstick skillet over medium-high heat until hot; coat the skillet with cooking spray. Add the onion and coat with cooking spray; cook 5 to 6 minutes or until beginning to turn a rich brown, stirring frequently. Remove from the skillet and set aside.

▶ Return the skillet to medium-high heat and recoat it with cooking spray. Sprinkle both sides of the beef with the steak seasoning and cook 2 minutes; turn and cook 1 minute or to desired doneness. Place on a plate and set aside. Add the onion to the skillet with the water and salt; bring to a boil and cook 15 seconds, stirring constantly. Top the steaks with the onion mixture and serve immediately for peak flavors.

Calories 170; total fat 4.5g (saturated fat 1.5g); protein 25g; carbohydrates 4g; fiber 1g; cholesterol 50mg; sodium 210mg; vitamin A 0%; vitamin C 4%; calcium 4%; iron 10%

COOK'S NOTE: *Do not overcook the beef or it will be tough.*

Excellent source of fiber and vitamins A and C

Good source of iron

Makes 4 steaks plus about ½ cup onion mixture total

Serves 4 *(3 ounces cooked beef, 2 tablespoons onion mixture, about 1 cup potatoes, and ¾ cup melon per serving)*

SERVE WITH

1 1-pound, 4-ounce package refrigerated diced potatoes with onions, cooked according to package instructions, but with only 1 tablespoon oil and ¼ teaspoon salt

Calories 140; total fat 3.5g (saturated fat 0g); protein 3g; carbohydrates 28g; fiber 3g; cholesterol 0mg; sodium 190mg; vitamin A 0%; vitamin C 2%; calcium 0%; iron 0%

3 cups diced honeydew

Calories 40; total fat 0g (saturated fat 0g); protein 1g; carbohydrates 10g; fiber 1g; cholesterol 0mg; sodium 20mg; vitamin A 80%; vitamin C 70%; calcium 2%; iron 2%

Sausage and Glazed Pineapple

with Toasted Waffles and Sour Cream

Calories 350; total fat 6g (saturated fat 1.5g); protein 13g; carbohydrates 65g; fiber 4g; cholesterol 25mg; sodium 640mg; vitamin A 20%; vitamin C 20%; calcium 10%; iron 15%

1 20-ounce can pineapple slices in juice, undrained

2 tablespoons packed dark brown sugar

2 tablespoons diet margarine

¼ teaspoon ground cinnamon

8 lean breakfast turkey sausage links

▶ Place eight pineapple slices and ¼ cup of the juice in a medium bowl. Store remaining pineapple and juice in the refrigerator for later use.

▶ Place a large nonstick skillet over medium-high heat; add the sugar, margarine, and cinnamon. When the margarine is melted, stir and add the pineapple slices (not the juice) in a single layer. Cook 5 minutes or until richly browned, turning frequently, and set aside on serving platter. Cover to keep warm, if desired.

▶ Coat the pan residue with cooking spray, and reduce heat to medium. Add the sausages and coat with cooking spray; cook 14 minutes or until the meat reaches 170°F, turning frequently, using two utensils for easy handling. (You may need to reduce the heat to medium low if the sausages are browning too quickly.) Place on a serving platter with the pineapple.

▶ Increase the heat to medium high, add the reserved ¼ cup juice, and cook 45 seconds or until it measures 2 tablespoons. Drizzle evenly over the sausage.

Calories 190; total fat 4g (saturated fat 1g); protein 7g; carbohydrates 35g; fiber 1g; cholesterol 15mg; sodium 360mg; vitamin A 6%; vitamin C 20%; calcium 2%; iron 4%

COOK'S NOTE: *The easiest way to accurately test the temperature of the sausage links is by inserting the tip of the thermometer into one end of the sausage.*

Excellent source of vitamins A and C

Good source of fiber, calcium, and iron

Makes 8 sausage links plus 8 pineapple slices total

Serves 4 *(2 sausage links, 2 pineapple slices, 1 waffle, 1 tablespoon syrup, and 3 tablespoons sour cream per serving)*

SERVE WITH

4 multibran frozen waffles, toasted and topped with 4 tablespoons light, reduced-calorie pancake syrup and ¾ cup fat-free sour cream or plain nonfat yogurt

Calories 160; total fat 2.5g (saturated fat 0.5g); protein 6g; carbohydrates 30g; fiber 3g; cholesterol 10mg; sodium 280mg; vitamin A 15%; vitamin C 0%; calcium 10%; iron 10%

Creamy Swiss and Ham Mini Bagels

with Orange Juice and Honeydew-Blueberry Bowls

Calories 350; total fat 4.5g (saturated fat 1.5g); protein 16g; carbohydrates 65g; fiber 7g; cholesterol 30mg; sodium 830mg; vitamin A 10%; vitamin C 180%; calcium 10%; iron 15%

1 cup (4 ounces) turkey ham, sliced thin and chopped fine

4 ¾-ounce wedges light Swiss cheese spread, such as Laughing Cow

½ to 1 teaspoon dried dill weed

4 mini whole-wheat bagels, halved and lightly toasted

▶ Combine the turkey ham, cheese spread, and dill in a medium bowl, and stir until well blended. Spoon equal amounts of the ham mixture on each bagel half.

Calories 190; total fat 4g (saturated fat 1.5g); protein 13g; carbohydrates 28g; fiber 4g; cholesterol 30mg; sodium 810mg; vitamin A 2%; vitamin C 0%; calcium 8%; iron 10%

TIME-SHAVER TIP: *Have the butcher slice the ham thin for you. Wrap it tightly with plastic wrap in smaller amounts and freeze it so you can have it on hand and already sliced.*

Excellent source of fiber and vitamin C

Good source of vitamin A, calcium, and iron

Makes 8 mini bagel halves total

Serves 4 *(2 mini bagel halves, ¾ cup juice, ¾ cup melon, and ⅓ cup blueberries per serving)*

SERVE WITH

3 cups orange juice

Calories 80; total fat 0.5g (saturated fat 0g); protein 1g; carbohydrates 19g; fiber 0g; cholesterol 0mg; sodium 0mg; vitamin A 6%; vitamin C 130%; calcium 2%; iron 2%

3 cups cubed honeydew mixed with 1⅓ cups fresh blueberries

Calories 70; total fat 0g (saturated fat 0g); protein 1g; carbohydrates 19g; fiber 2g; cholesterol 0mg; sodium 25mg; vitamin A 2%; vitamin C 45%; calcium 2%; iron 2%

Broccoli-Bacon Frittata

with Fresh Oranges, Wheat Bagels, and Herbed Cream Cheese

Calories 340; total fat 7g (saturated fat 2.5g); protein 22g; carbohydrates 51g; fiber 13g; cholesterol 15mg; sodium 890mg; vitamin A 40%; vitamin C 180%; calcium 10%; iron 25%

8 bacon slices, chopped

2 cups (6 ounces) small broccoli florets

⅓ cup water

¼ teaspoon salt

1½ cups egg substitute with vegetables and herbs

2 medium plum tomatoes, sliced thin (1 cup)

2 medium green onions, chopped fine (¼ cup)

▸ Place a medium nonstick skillet over medium-high heat until hot. Add the bacon and cook until crisp, stirring frequently. Drain on paper towels and set aside.

▸ Dry the skillet with a paper towel; add the broccoli and water. Bring to a boil over medium-high heat; reduce heat, cover, and simmer 1½ minutes or until tender crisp. Drain well.

▸ Place the skillet over medium-low heat and coat with cooking spray. Return the broccoli to the skillet in an even layer, sprinkle with ⅛ teaspoon of the salt, and carefully pour the egg substitute evenly over all. Arrange the tomato slices evenly on top, cover, and cook 10 minutes or until the eggs are almost set. Remove from heat, sprinkle with the remaining ⅛ teaspoon salt, and top with the bacon and onion. Place on a plate and cut into wedges.

Calories 160; total fat 1.5g (saturated fat 0.5g); protein 7g; carbohydrates 31g; fiber 5g; cholesterol 0mg; sodium 300mg; vitamin A 0%; vitamin C 0%; calcium 2%; iron 10%

TIME-SHAVER TIP: *Cut-up broccoli can be purchased in the produce section of most supermarkets, but be sure to cut the broccoli into smaller pieces for best results.*

Excellent source of fiber, vitamins A and C, and iron

Good source of calcium

Makes 1 9-inch frittata total

Serves 4 (¼ *frittata, 1 orange, ½ bagel, and 1 teaspoon cheese spread per serving*)

SERVE WITH

4 medium oranges

Calories 60; total fat 0g (saturated fat 0g); protein 1g; carbohydrates 15g; fiber 3g; cholesterol 0mg; sodium 0mg; vitamin A 6%; vitamin C 120%; calcium 6%; iron 0%

2 whole-wheat bagels, halved and toasted, topped with 4 teaspoons light herb and garlic cream cheese, such as Boursin

Calories 120; total fat 5g (saturated fat 2g); protein 14g; carbohydrates 5g; fiber 1g; cholesterol 10mg; sodium 590mg; vitamin A 35%; vitamin C 60%; calcium 6%; iron 10%

Knife-and-Fork Breakfast Tortillas

with Chilled Orange Juice and Banana Slices

Calories 350; total fat 5g (saturated fat 2.5g); protein 21g; carbohydrates 55g; fiber 5g; cholesterol 15mg; sodium 640mg; vitamin A 30%; vitamin C 190%; calcium 25%; iron 15%

4 soft soft corn tortillas

1 medium green bell pepper, chopped fine (1 cup)

2 cups egg substitute, plain or with peppers and onions

½ cup (2 ounces) finely shredded reduced-fat sharp cheddar cheese

½ cup fat-free sour cream

½ cup picante sauce

1 medium lime, quartered

► Heat the tortillas, one at a time, over a medium gas flame or directly on electric coils, turning every few seconds until hot and toasty, about 15 to 20 seconds. Wrap in foil to keep warm and absorb the smoky flavors.

► Heat a large nonstick skillet over medium heat, and coat the skillet with cooking spray. Add the bell pepper and coat with cooking spray; cook 3 minutes or until tender crisp, stirring frequently. Add the egg substitute and cook 1 to 2 minutes, lifting up the egg mixture to allow raw portions to cook to achieve a scrambled egg effect.

▶ Arrange a tortilla on each of four plates, spoon equal amounts of the egg mixture on top of the tortillas, sprinkle the cheese evenly over all of them, and spoon 2 tablespoons of the sour cream and picante sauce on top of each. Squeeze lime juice over all four servings.

Calories 210; total fat 4.5g (saturated fat 2.5g); protein 19g; carbohydrates 23g; fiber 3g; cholesterol 15mg; sodium 640mg; vitamin A 25%; vitamin C 50%; calcium 20%; iron 15%

COOK'S NOTE: *Be sure to "toast" the tortillas first to give another layer of flavor to your dish.*

Excellent source of vitamins A and C, calcium, and fiber

Good source of iron

Makes 4 filled tortillas total

Serves 4 *(1 filled tortilla, ¾ cup juice, and ½ medium banana per serving)*

SERVE WITH

3 cups orange juice

Calories 80; total fat 0.5g (saturated fat 0g); protein 1g; carbohydrates 19g; fiber 0g; cholesterol 0mg; sodium 0mg; vitamin A 6%; vitamin C 130%; calcium 2%; iron 2%

2 medium bananas, peeled and sliced (2 cups)

Calories 50; total fat 0g (saturated fat 0g); protein 1g; carbohydrates 13g; fiber 2g; cholesterol 0mg; sodium 0mg; vitamin A 0%; vitamin C 8%; calcium 0%; iron 0%

Country Garden Frittata

with Olive-Oiled Country French Bread and Vegetable Juice

Calories 350; total fat 12g (saturated fat 3.5g); protein 21g; carbohydrates 41g; fiber 5g; cholesterol 25mg; sodium 850mg; vitamin A 60%; vitamin C 190%; calcium 15%; iron 20%

3 ounces bulk 50% less-fat pork sausage, such as Jimmy Dean

1 medium green bell pepper, chopped (1 cup)

½ medium yellow onion, chopped (½ cup)

1 cup egg substitute

1 teaspoon Worcestershire sauce

¼ teaspoon salt

1½ cups (8 ounces) frozen corn kernels, thawed

⅓ cup (1½ ounces) finely shredded reduced-fat sharp cheddar cheese

▶ Heat a medium nonstick skillet over medium heat until hot, and coat the skillet with cooking spray. Add the sausage and cook until browned, stirring frequently. Set aside on a separate plate.

▶ Coat the pan residue with cooking spray. Add the bell pepper and onion; coat the vegetables with cooking spray and cook 6 minutes or until beginning to turn a rich brown, stirring frequently.

▶ Meanwhile, in a small bowl, combine the egg substitute, Worcestershire sauce, and salt. Reduce the heat to medium low, add the corn to the pepper mixture, and stir until well blended. Gently pour the egg mixture evenly over all; cover and cook 10 minutes or until just set in the center. Remove from heat, sprinkle evenly with the cheese, and sprinkle the sausage over all. Cover and let stand 2 minutes to allow the cheese to melt.

Calories 200; total fat 7g (saturated fat 3g); protein 18g; carbohydrates 19g; fiber 2g; cholesterol 25mg; sodium 580mg; vitamin A 35%; vitamin C 120%; calcium 10%; iron 10%

TIME-SHAVER TIP: *To thaw corn (or other frozen vegetables) quickly, place in a colander and run under cold water about 20 seconds; shake off excess liquid before using.*

Excellent source of vitamins A and C and fiber

Good source of calcium and iron

Makes 1 9-inch frittata total

Serves 4 *(¼ frittata, 1 slice bread, 1 teaspoon oil, and ¾ cup juice per serving)*

SERVE WITH

4 ounces country French bread, cut into 4 slices, lightly toasted, and drizzled with 4 teaspoons extra-virgin olive oil

Calories 120; total fat 5g (saturated fat 0.5g); protein 2g; carbohydrates 14g; fiber 1g; cholesterol 0mg; sodium 180mg; vitamin A 0%; vitamin C 0%; calcium 2%; iron 4%

3 cups low-sodium vegetable juice

Calories 35; total fat 0g (saturated fat 0g); protein 1g; carbohydrates 8g; fiber 1g; cholesterol 0mg; sodium 100mg; vitamin A 30%; vitamin C 70%; calcium 2%; iron 2%

Mini Ham and Potato Quiches

with Tomato and Avocado Slices, and Citrus Juice Blend

Calories 340; total fat 13g (saturated fat 4g); protein 19g; carbohydrates 35g; fiber 5g; cholesterol 35mg; sodium 860mg; vitamin A 90%; vitamin C 120%; calcium 20%; iron 10%

1 cup egg substitute

2 cups refrigerated shredded potatoes

4 medium green onions, chopped fine (½ cup)

1 cup (4 ounces) extra-lean turkey ham, sliced thin and chopped

3 ¾-ounce wedges Swiss cheese spread, such as Laughing Cow, cut into small pieces

½ cup (2 ounces) shredded reduced-fat sharp cheddar cheese

▶ Preheat the oven to 350°F.

▶ Coat a 12-cup nonstick muffin tin with cooking spray and set aside.

▶ Combine all of the ingredients, except the cheddar cheese, and stir until blended. Spoon equal amounts of the egg mixture into each of the muffin cups and bake 15 minutes or until eggs are just set. Sprinkle evenly with the cheddar cheese, and bake 2 minutes or until cheese melts.

▶ Remove from the oven and cool on a rack 5 minutes before serving.

Calories 170; total fat 6g (saturated fat 3g); protein 18g; carbohydrates 10g; fiber 1g; cholesterol 35mg; sodium 820mg; vitamin A 10%; vitamin C 8%; calcium 20%; iron 8%

COOK'S NOTE: *This dish is ideal for buffet entertaining; it's easy to make and pretty to serve.*

Excellent source of fiber, vitamins A and C, and calcium

Good source of iron

Makes 12 mini quiches total

Serves 4 *(3 mini quiches, ½ cup tomato slices, ¼ cup avocado slices, and ¾ cup juice per serving)*

SERVE WITH

2 medium tomatoes, sliced (2 cups)

Calories 10; total fat 0g (saturated fat 0g); protein 0g; carbohydrates 2g; fiber 1g; cholesterol 0mg; sodium 0mg; vitamin A 10%; vitamin C 10%; calcium 0%; iron 0%

1 ripe medium avocado, sliced (1 cup)

Calories 80; total fat 7g (saturated fat 1g); protein 1g; carbohydrates 4g; fiber 3g; cholesterol 0mg; sodium 0mg; vitamin A 2%; vitamin C 8%; calcium 0%; iron 2%

3 cups citrus juice blend, such as V8 VFusion

Calories 80; total fat 0g (saturated fat 0g); protein 0g; carbohydrates 19g; fiber 0g; cholesterol 0mg; sodium 35mg; vitamin A 70%; vitamin C 90%; calcium 0%; iron 0%

English Muffin Pizza Scramble

with Tropical Fruit Juice and Nectarine Slices

Calories 350; total fat 10g (saturated fat 4g); protein 23g; carbohydrates 46g; fiber 5g; cholesterol 25mg; sodium 970mg; vitamin A 15%; vitamin C 80%; calcium 30%; iron 15%

4 whole-wheat English muffins, halved

1 cup egg substitute

1 teaspoon dried oregano leaves

⅛ teaspoon dried pepper flakes

½ cup pizza sauce

16 small turkey pepperoni slices

1 cup (4 ounces) shredded mozzarella cheese

1 tablespoon grated Parmesan cheese

► Preheat the broiler.

► Place muffin halves on a baking pan and broil 1½ to 2 minutes on each side or until lightly toasted, watching closely so they don't burn. Remove from the broiler and set aside. Do not turn off the broiler.

► Heat a medium nonstick skillet over medium heat until hot, and coat the skillet with cooking spray. Add the egg substitute, sprinkle with the oregano and pepper flakes, and cook 2 minutes, stirring occasionally. Remove from heat.

► In this order, top the muffin halves with equal amounts of sauce, pepperoni, eggs, and mozzarella. Broil 1 minute or until cheese is melted and beginning to brown very lightly. Remove from the broiler, and sprinkle with the Parmesan.

Calories 290; total fat 10g (saturated fat 4g); protein 22g; carbohydrates 31g; fiber 4g; cholesterol 25mg; sodium 930mg; vitamin A 15%; vitamin C 2%; calcium 30%; iron 15%

COOK'S NOTE: *Broiling the muffins on both sides makes a crisper crust.*

Excellent source of fiber, vitamin C, and calcium

Good source of vitamin A and iron

Makes 8 muffin pizzas total

Serves 4 *(2 muffin pizzas, ¾ cup juice, ½ cup ginger ale, and about ½ cup nectarine slices per serving)*

SERVE WITH

3 cups light orange, strawberry, and banana juice mixed with 2 cups diet ginger ale

Calories 25; total fat 0g (saturated fat 0g); protein 1g; carbohydrates 7g; fiber 0g; cholesterol 0mg; sodium 35mg; vitamin A 0%; vitamin C 70%; calcium 0%; iron 0%

2 medium nectarines or peaches, pitted and sliced (2 cups)

Calories 35; total fat 0g (saturated fat 0g); protein 1g; carbohydrates 8g; fiber 1g; cholesterol 0mg; sodium 0mg; vitamin A 2%; vitamin C 8%; calcium 0%; iron 2%

Bacon and Egg Breakfast Sandwich

with Orange Juice Fizzer and Peach Yogurt

Calories 350; total fat 7g (saturated fat 2.5g); protein 23g; carbohydrates 52g; fiber 8g; cholesterol 25mg; sodium 870mg; vitamin A 20%; vitamin C 130%; calcium 35%; iron 15%

8 low-sodium bacon slices

1 cup egg substitute

3 tablespoons fat-free milk

¼ to ½ teaspoon Louisiana hot sauce

8 reduced-calorie whole-wheat bread slices, toasted

4 ¾-ounce wedges light Swiss cheese spread, such as Laughing Cow

1 medium tomato, cut into 4 slices (4 ounces)

▶ Heat a large nonstick skillet over medium-high heat until hot. Add the bacon and cook until crisp. Drain on paper towels and blot dry; discard any bacon drippings.

▶ Meanwhile, combine the egg substitute, milk, and hot sauce in a small bowl, and stir until well blended.

▶ Heat the skillet over medium heat, and coat the skillet with cooking spray. Add the egg mixture and cook 1 to 2 minutes, lifting up the egg mixture to allow raw portions to cook to achieve a scrambled egg effect. Remove from heat.

Makes 4 sandwiches total

Serves 4 (2 sandwich halves, ¾ cup juice, ½ cup ginger ale, and 4 ounces yogurt per serving)

▶ Spread one side of each bread slice with the cheese spread. Top four of the bread slices with tomato slices, bacon slices, and equal amounts of the scrambled egg mixture, top with the remaining four bread slices (cheese side down), and cut in half.

Calories 210; total fat 7g (saturated fat 2.5g); protein 17g; carbohydrates 23g; fiber 8g; cholesterol 20mg; sodium 810mg; vitamin A 15%; vitamin C 10%; calcium 15%; iron 15%

TIME-SHAVER TIP: *Toast the bread slices while the bacon is cooking and cover with foil to keep warm. For a crunchier toast, let stand at room temperature and do not cover with foil.*

Excellent source of fiber, vitamins A and C, and calcium

Good source of iron

SERVE WITH

3 cups orange juice mixed with 2 cups diet ginger ale

Calories 70; total fat 0g (saturated fat 0g); protein 1g; carbohydrates 17g; fiber 0g; cholesterol 0mg; sodium 0mg; vitamin A 4%; vitamin C 120%; calcium 2%; iron 2%

4 4-ounce snack packs nonfat/light peach-flavored yogurt sweetened with aspartame

Calories 60; total fat 0g (saturated fat 0g); protein 4g; carbohydrates 11g; fiber 0g; cholesterol 0mg; sodium 65mg; vitamin A 0%; vitamin C 2%; calcium 15%; iron 0%

Fried Eggs on Rice and Black Beans

with Fresh Mango and Pineapple

Calories 350; total fat 10g (saturated fat 2g); protein 14g; carbohydrates 51g; fiber 8g; cholesterol 210mg; sodium 520mg; vitamin A 30%; vitamin C 130%; calcium 6%; iron 15%

1½ cups water

¾ cup dry quick-cooking brown rice

½ teaspoon chili powder

½ medium red bell pepper, chopped fine (½ cup)

¼ medium green bell pepper, chopped fine (¼ cup)

½ 15-ounce can black beans, rinsed and drained

1 tablespoon extra-virgin olive oil

½ teaspoon salt

4 large eggs

1 medium lime, cut into wedges

Hot pepper sauce, optional

▶ Combine the water, rice, and chili powder in a medium saucepan and cook according to package directions, omitting any salt or fat.

▶ Meanwhile, heat a large nonstick skillet over medium-high heat until hot, and coat the skillet with cooking spray. Add the bell peppers, coat them with cooking spray, and cook 3 minutes or until just tender, stirring frequently. Stir the beans into the peppers and set aside.

▶ When the rice is cooked, add the bean mixture to the rice. Add 2 teaspoons of the oil and all but ⅛ teaspoon of the salt. Cover and set aside.

▶ Dry the skillet with a paper towel and place over medium heat; coat the skillet with cooking spray and add the remaining 1 teaspoon oil. Tilt the skillet to coat the bottom lightly. Add the eggs, one at a time, and cook 1 minute; turn and cook 30 seconds to 1 minute or to desired doneness. (For easy turning, coat a spatula with cooking spray each time.) Sprinkle with the remaining ⅛ teaspoon salt. Place on top of the rice mixture. Serve with lime and hot sauce.

Calories 300; total fat 10g (saturated fat 2g); protein 13g; carbohydrates 37g; fiber 6g; cholesterol 210mg; sodium 520mg; vitamin A 20%; vitamin C 80%; calcium 6%; iron 15%

TIME-SHAVER TIP: *This is a great way to use leftover cooked rice; you will need 2 cups.*

Excellent source of fiber and vitamins A and C

Good source of iron

Makes 4 eggs and 3 cups rice mixture total

Serves 4 *(1 egg, ¾ cup rice mixture, and ½ cup mango-pineapple mixture per serving)*

SERVE WITH

1 medium mango, peeled and cubed (1 cup), and tossed with 1 cup diced fresh pineapple

Calories 50; total fat 0g (saturated fat 0g); protein 0g; carbohydrates 14g; fiber 1g; cholesterol 0mg; sodium 0mg; vitamin A 8%; vitamin C 45%; calcium 2%; iron 0%

Drop Biscuits and Creamy Apricot Spread

with Smoked Sausage, Fresh Oranges, and Cold Milk

Calories 350; total fat 4.5g (saturated fat 1.5g); protein 18g; carbohydrates 63g; fiber 4g; cholesterol 15mg; sodium 1,000mg; vitamin A 20%; vitamin C 120%; calcium 35%; iron 15%

1½ cups healthy variety pancake and baking mix, such as Bisquick Heart Smart

⅔ cup 1% fat buttermilk

2 teaspoons apricot fruit spread

2 tablespoons diet margarine

¼ teaspoon vanilla extract

▶ Preheat the oven to 450°F.

▶ Combine the baking mix and buttermilk in a medium bowl, and stir until just blended. Spoon onto an ungreased, nonstick cookie sheet in eight mounds, about 2 inches apart. Bake 8 minutes or until lightly golden.

▶ Meanwhile, place the fruit spread in a small microwave-safe bowl and cook on High for 10 seconds or until slightly melted. Remove from the microwave, add the margarine and vanilla, and stir with a fork until well blended. It may be a bit lumpy at this point.

▶ Using a serrated knife, split the biscuits in half crosswise, and spoon equal amounts of the apricot mixture on top of each.

Calories 160; total fat 3g (saturated fat 1g); protein 4g; carbohydrates 29g; fiber 1g; cholesterol 5mg; sodium 530mg; vitamin A 6%; vitamin C 0%; calcium 4%; iron 6%

TIME-SHAVER TIP: *Fresh orange sections are sold in the produce section of your supermarket. If desired, substitute ⅓ cup orange sections for each of the whole oranges.*

Excellent source of vitamins A and C and calcium

Good source of fiber and iron

Makes 8 biscuits and 3 tablespoons fruit spread total

Serves 4 *(2 biscuits, 2 teaspoons fruit spread mixture, 1½ ounces sausage, 1 orange, and 1 cup milk per serving)*

SERVE WITH

6 ounces smoked turkey sausage, halved lengthwise, cut into 2-inch pieces, and browned

Calories 45; total fat 1g (saturated fat 0g); protein 3g; carbohydrates 5g; fiber 0g; cholesterol 10mg; sodium 340mg; vitamin A 0%; vitamin C 2%; calcium 0%; iron 6%

4 medium oranges

Calories 60; total fat 0g (saturated fat 0g); protein 1g; carbohydrates 15g; fiber 3g; cholesterol 0mg; sodium 0mg; vitamin A 6%; vitamin C 120%; calcium 6%; iron 0%

4 cups fat-free milk

Calories 90; total fat 0g (saturated fat 0g); protein 9g; carbohydrates 13g; fiber 0g; cholesterol 5mg; sodium 130mg; vitamin A 10%; vitamin C 2%; calcium 25%; iron 0%

Rustic Breakfast Roll-Ups

with Sweet Mango and Kiwi

Calories 350; total fat 9g (saturated fat 3.5g); protein 19g; carbohydrates 51g; fiber 9g; cholesterol 20mg; sodium 980mg; vitamin A 15%; vitamin C 80%; calcium 40%; iron 10%

⅔ cup picante sauce

2 teaspoons extra-virgin olive oil

1 cup fat-free refried beans

8 soft corn tortillas

½ teaspoon ground cumin, optional

8 ¾-ounce pieces reduced-fat string cheese

▶ Preheat the oven to 400°F.

▶ In a small bowl, combine ⅓ cup of the picante sauce with the oil and set aside.

▶ Coat a large, foil-lined baking pan with cooking spray.

▶ Using a fork, spread the beans evenly over each tortilla. Sprinkle with cumin, top with cheese, roll loosely, and place seam side down on baking pan. Spoon the picante-and-oil mixture evenly over all and bake, uncovered, 18 to 20 minutes or until cheese melts. Spoon the remaining ⅓ cup picante-and-oil mixture over all.

Calories 300; total fat 9g (saturated fat 3.5g); protein 18g; carbohydrates 37g; fiber 7g; cholesterol 20mg; sodium 980mg; vitamin A 6%; vitamin C 0%; calcium 35%; iron 8%

COOK'S NOTE: *The tortillas may split slightly while rolling, which is characteristic of soft soft corn tortillas.*

Excellent source of fiber, vitamin C, and calcium

Good source of vitamin A and iron

Makes 8 roll-ups total

Serves 4 *(2 roll-ups and about ½ cup fruit mixture per serving)*

SERVE WITH

1 medium mango, peeled and cubed (1 cup), and 2 kiwifruit, peeled and diced (about 1 cup)

Calories 60; total fat 0g (saturated fat 0g); protein 1g; carbohydrates 14g; fiber 2g; cholesterol 0mg; sodium 0mg; vitamin A 8%; vitamin C 80%; calcium 2%; iron 2%

Baquette Cheese Toast

with a Sauté of Red and Green Peppers

Calories 340; total fat 9g (saturated fat 3.5g); protein 27g; carbohydrates 33g; fiber 5g; cholesterol 45mg; sodium 580mg; vitamin A 45%; vitamin C 200%; calcium 20%; iron 10%

8 ounces whole-grain or regular baguette, cut in half lengthwise and cut into 8 pieces

1 garlic clove, halved, optional

1 tablespoon plus 1 teaspoon dijonnaise

1 tablespoon plus 1 teaspoon diet mayonnaise

1 cup cooked, diced chicken breast, optional

1 cup (4 ounces) reduced-fat grated four-cheese blend, such as Sargento

3 medium plum tomatoes, chopped (about 1½ cups)

▶ Preheat the broiler.

▶ Line a cookie sheet with foil and arrange the bread on the foil. Broil 45 to 60 seconds on each side, watching closely so it doesn't burn. Remove from the broiler.

▶ Rub the garlic evenly over the top of each slice of the bread, if desired. Combine the dijonnaise and mayonnaise in a small bowl; spread evenly over each slice and top with equal amounts of chicken (if desired) and cheese; broil 1½ to 2 minutes or until the cheese melts and the edges are beginning to brown lightly.

▶ Remove from the broiler, and sprinkle evenly with the tomatoes.

Calories 320; total fat 9g (saturated fat 3.5g); protein 26g; carbohydrates 29g; fiber 4g; cholesterol 45mg; sodium 580mg; vitamin A 15%; vitamin C 10%; calcium 20%; iron 10%

TIME-SHAVER TIP: *This is a great way to take advantage of day-old French bread.*

Excellent source of fiber, vitamins A and C, and calcium

Good source of iron

Makes 8 cheese toasts total

Serves 4 *(2 bread slices and ½ cup sautéed peppers per serving)*

SERVE WITH

1 medium red bell pepper, sliced (1 cup), and 1 medium green bell pepper, sliced (1 cup), sautéed quickly with cooking spray

Calories 20; total fat 0g (saturated fat 0g); protein 1g; carbohydrates 5g; fiber 2g; cholesterol 0mg; sodium 0mg; vitamin A 30%; vitamin C 190%; calcium 0%; iron 2%

Cinnamon French Toast with Cheesecake Sauce

with Canadian Bacon Slices

Calories 350; total fat 11g (saturated fat 3.5g); protein 21g; carbohydrates 40g; fiber 4g; cholesterol 25mg; sodium 850mg; vitamin A 15%; vitamin C 80%; calcium 10%; iron 30%

2 cups whole strawberries, quartered

2 tablespoons pourable sugar substitute, such as Splenda

6 tablespoons (3 ounces) light cream cheese, tub style, softened

¼ cup fat-free sour cream

½ teaspoon vanilla extract

2 teaspoons canola oil

1 cup egg substitute

8 slices raisin cinnamon bread

> Combine the strawberries and 1 tablespoon of the sugar substitute in a medium bowl; toss gently and set aside.

> In a small bowl, whisk together the remaining sugar substitute, cream cheese, sour cream, and vanilla until smooth.

> Place a large nonstick skillet over medium heat until hot. Coat the skillet with cooking spray, add 1 teaspoon of the oil, and tilt the skillet to coat the bottom lightly.

> Pour the egg substitute into a 13″ × 9″ baking pan. Add the bread slices and turn several times to coat evenly. Place four of the bread slices in the skillet and cook 3 minutes on each side or until golden. Set aside on a separate plate; cover to keep warm. Repeat with the remaining oil and bread slices.

Calories 300; total fat 9g (saturated fat 2.5g); protein 15g; carbohydrates 40g; fiber 4g; cholesterol 10mg; sodium 450mg; vitamin A 15%; vitamin C 80%; calcium 10%; iron 30%

TIME-SHAVER TIP: *Soften the cream cheese in the microwave on High for 10 seconds.*

Excellent source of vitamin C and iron

Good source of fiber, vitamin A, and calcium

Makes 8 toast slices, 2 cups berries, and ½ cup sauce total

Serves 4 *(2 toast slices, ½ cup berries, 2 tablespoons sauce, and 2 bacon slices per serving)*

SERVE WITH

4 slices Canadian bacon (4 ounces total), halved crosswise and browned

Calories 45; total fat 2g (saturated fat 0.5g); protein 6g; carbohydrates 0g; fiber 0g; cholesterol 15mg; sodium 400mg; vitamin A 0%; vitamin C 0%; calcium 0%; iron 2%

Light "Italian" Toast with Fresh Citrus Sauce

with Skillet-Fried Turkey Bacon

Calories 350; total fat 12g (saturated fat 2.5g); protein 16g; carbohydrates 45g; fiber 2g; cholesterol 25mg; sodium 850mg; vitamin A 15%; vitamin C 45%; calcium 8%; iron 20%

1½ cups egg substitute

2 teaspoons canola oil

8 ounces Italian bread, cut diagonally into 8 slices (about
   1 inch wide each)

½ teaspoon grated orange rind

1 cup orange juice

3 tablespoons sugar

2 teaspoons cornstarch

2 tablespoons diet margarine

½ teaspoon vanilla extract

▶ Preheat the oven to 200°F.

▶ Pour the egg substitute into a shallow bowl and set aside.

▶ Place a large nonstick skillet over medium heat until hot. Add
   1 teaspoon of the oil and tilt the skillet to coat the bottom
   lightly. Dip four bread slices into the egg substitute and cook
   4 minutes on each side or until golden. Place on a plate and
   put in the oven to keep warm while repeating the process
   with the remaining oil and bread slices.

▶ Meanwhile, combine the orange rind, juice, sugar, and
   cornstarch in a small saucepan. Whisk together until the
   cornstarch has completely dissolved. Bring to a boil over

medium-high heat and boil 1 minute, stirring frequently. Remove from heat and stir in the margarine and vanilla until the margarine has melted. Serve the sauce over the bread slices.

Calories 280; total fat 7g (saturated fat 1g); protein 11g; carbohydrates 44g; fiber 2g; cholesterol 0mg; sodium 500mg; vitamin A 15%; vitamin C 45%; calcium 8%; iron 15%

COOK'S NOTE: *Some markets make whole-wheat Italian bread. Check the labels for the amount of fiber they contain; the desired number is 2 grams of dietary fiber per serving.*

Excellent source of vitamin C and iron

Good source of vitamin A

Makes 8 Italian toasts and 1 cup sauce total

Serves 4 *(2 toasts, ¼ cup sauce, and 2 bacon slices per serving)*

SERVE WITH

8 slices turkey bacon, crisp cooked

Calories 70; total fat 6g (saturated fat 1.5g); protein 4g; carbohydrates 0g; fiber 0g; cholesterol 25mg; sodium 340mg; vitamin A 0%; vitamin C 0%; calcium 2%; iron 2%

Peach-Cranberry Pancakes

with Skillet Bacon

Calories 340; total fat 12g (saturated fat 3g); protein 14g; carbohydrates 50g; fiber 6g; cholesterol 35mg; sodium 940mg; vitamin A 15%; vitamin C 6%; calcium 25%; iron 20%

1 cup fresh, or frozen and thawed, sliced peaches

½ cup dried cranberries

¼ cup water

¼ cup diet margarine

2 tablespoons packed dark brown sugar

½ teaspoon ground cinnamon

1 cup healthy variety pancake and baking mix, such as
   Bisquick Heart Smart

¼ cup wheat germ

¾ cup plus 2 tablespoons fat-free milk

▶ Preheat the oven to 200°F.

▶ Combine the peaches, cranberries, and water in a microwave-safe bowl, cover with plastic wrap, and microwave on High for 3 minutes. Stir in the margarine, sugar, and cinnamon, and set aside.

▶ Combine the baking mix, wheat germ, and milk in a medium bowl, and stir until blended.

▶ Heat a large nonstick skillet over medium heat until hot. In scant ¼-cup amounts, pour the batter into the skillet and cook 2 minutes or until tops are bubbly and edges are dry; turn and cook 2 minutes or until golden on the bottom. Place the pancakes on a plate, put them in the oven to keep warm, and repeat with the remaining batter. Serve equal amounts of the peach mixture on top of each serving.

Calories 260; total fat 6g (saturated fat 1.5g); protein 9g; carbohydrates 49g; fiber 6g; cholesterol 10mg; sodium 600mg; vitamin A 15%; vitamin C 6%; calcium 25%; iron 20%

COOK'S NOTE: *This is a very rich-tasting topping. Serve it over French toast or waffles as well.*

Excellent source of fiber, calcium, and iron

Good source of vitamin A

Makes 8 pancakes plus 1¼ cups peach mixture total

Serves 4 *(2 pancakes, about ⅓ cup peach mixture, and 2 bacon slices per serving)*

SERVE WITH

8 slices turkey bacon, crisp cooked

Calories 70; total fat 6g (saturated fat 1.5g); protein 4g; carbohydrates 0g; fiber 0g; cholesterol 25mg; sodium 340mg; vitamin A 0%; vitamin C 0%; calcium 2%; iron 2%

Mushroom and Red Pepper Cheese-Smothered Grits

with Scrambled Eggs, Honeyed English Muffins, and Melon Wedges

Calories 350; total fat 7g (saturated fat 4 g); protein 23g; carbohydrates 49g; fiber 5g; cholesterol 20mg; sodium 870mg; vitamin A 90%; vitamin C 190%; calcium 30%; iron 20%

2½ cups water

½ cup quick-cooking grits

½ 8-ounce package sliced mushrooms (1½ cups)

1 medium red bell pepper, chopped (1 cup)

4 medium green onions, chopped (½ cup)

2 medium garlic cloves, minced

½ teaspoon Worcestershire sauce

½ teaspoon salt

1 cup (4 ounces) shredded reduced-fat sharp cheddar cheese

Coarsely ground black pepper to taste

▶ Bring the water to a boil in a medium skillet over high heat. Stir in the grits and cook according to the directions on the package, omitting any salt or fat.

▶ Meanwhile, heat a medium nonstick skillet over medium-high heat until hot, and coat the skillet with cooking spray. Add the mushrooms, coat them with cooking spray, and cook

3 minutes or until they begin to brown lightly. Add the bell pepper and all but 2 tablespoons of the onion; cook 4 minutes or until the pepper is just tender, stirring frequently. Add the garlic, Worcestershire sauce, and ¼ teaspoon of the salt; cook 30 seconds.

▶ When the grits are cooked, stir in the remaining ¼ teaspoon salt and place in a shallow serving bowl. Sprinkle the cheese evenly over all and top with the vegetables. Sprinkle with black pepper and the remaining onion.

Calories 210; total fat 7g (saturated fat 4g); protein 11g; carbohydrates 26g; fiber 2g; cholesterol 20mg; sodium 550mg; vitamin A 35%; vitamin C 140%; calcium 25%; iron 6%

COOK'S NOTE: Serve immediately or let stand 5 minutes to allow the cheese to melt and flavors to absorb.

Excellent source of fiber, vitamins A and C, calcium, and iron

---

Makes 2 cups grits plus 1 cup vegetables total

Serves 4 *(½ cup grits, ¼ cup vegetables, about ½ cup scrambled eggs, ½ English muffin, ½ teaspoon honey, and ⅛ cantaloupe per serving)*

SERVE WITH

1½ cups egg substitute, scrambled

Calories 45; total fat 0g (saturated fat 0g); protein 9g; carbohydrates 1g; fiber 0g; cholesterol 0mg; sodium 190mg; vitamin A 8%; vitamin C 0%; calcium 2%; iron 10%

2 whole-wheat English muffins, halved, toasted, and drizzled with 2 teaspoons honey

Calories 80; total fat 1g (saturated fat 0g); protein 3g; carbohydrates 16g; fiber 2g; cholesterol 0mg; sodium 120mg; vitamin A 0%; vitamin C 0%; calcium 2%; iron 4%

½ medium cantaloupe, cut into 8 wedges

Calories 25; total fat 0g (saturated fat 0g); protein 1g; carbohydrates 6g; fiber 1g; cholesterol 0mg; sodium 10mg; vitamin A 45%; vitamin C 40%; calcium 0%; iron 0%

Apple-Honey Oatmeal

with Cold Milk

Calories 350; total fat 5g (saturated fat 1g); protein 13g; carbohydrates 65g; fiber 6g; cholesterol 0mg; sodium 140mg; vitamin A 10%; vitamin C 6%; calcium 20%; iron 15%

3¼ cups water

¼ teaspoon salt

1¾ cups quick-cooking oats

1 medium apple, such as Gala (peeled, if desired), chopped (1 cup)

½ cup golden raisins

2 tablespoons wheat germ

¼ cup honey or maple syrup

1 tablespoon diet margarine

1½ teaspoons apple pie spice or ground cinnamon

1 teaspoon vanilla extract

▶ Bring the water and salt to a full boil in a large saucepan over high heat. Stir in the oats, apple, raisins, and wheat germ. Reduce heat to medium and cook, uncovered, 6 minutes or until thickened, stirring occasionally.

▶ Remove from heat, and stir in the remaining ingredients.

Calories 290; total fat 5g (saturated fat 1g); protein 7g; carbohydrates 56g; fiber 6g; cholesterol 0mg; sodium 50mg; vitamin A 6%; vitamin C 4%; calcium 4%; iron 15%

TIME-SHAVER TIP: *Substitute frozen diced peaches for the apple, if desired.*

Excellent source of fiber and calcium

Good source of vitamin A and iron

Makes 4 cups oatmeal total

Serves 4 *(1 cup oatmeal and ¾ cup milk per serving)*

SERVE WITH

3 cups fat-free milk

Calories 60; total fat 0g (saturated fat 0g); protein 6g; carbohydrates 9g; fiber 0g; cholesterol 0mg; sodium 90mg; vitamin A 6%; vitamin C 2%; calcium 15%; iron 0%

Fresh Berry Oatmeal with Sweet Cream

with Canadian Bacon Slices

Calories 340; total fat 6g (saturated fat 1.5g); protein 19g; carbohydrates 50g; fiber 7g; cholesterol 30mg; sodium 850mg; vitamin A 6%; vitamin C 40%; calcium 10%; iron 15%

1 cup fat-free half-and-half

3 tablespoons sugar

1 teaspoon vanilla extract

3 cups water

Dash of salt

1½ cups quick-cooking oats

1 teaspoon ground cinnamon

3 cups fresh berries

> Combine the half-and-half with the sugar in a small saucepan and cook over medium-high heat until bubbles form around the outer edges. Do not bring to a boil. Immediately remove from heat; stir in the vanilla and set aside.

> Bring the water and salt to a boil in a large saucepan over high heat. Stir in the oats; reduce heat to medium and cook 1 minute or until thickened. Stir in the cinnamon.

> To serve, spoon equal amounts of the oatmeal into each of four shallow soup bowls, pour the cream sauce over the oatmeal, and top with the berries.

Calories 260; total fat 2.5g (saturated fat 0g); protein 7g; carbohydrates 49g; fiber 7g; cholesterol 0mg; sodium 50mg; vitamin A 6%; vitamin C 40%; calcium 10%; iron 10%

COOK'S NOTE: *Use fresh berries when in season for peak flavor. Berries are now sold year-round in the supermarket, but they may not be as sweet. Add 1 to 2 teaspoons pourable sugar substitute to the berries before topping the oatmeal, if desired.*

Excellent source of fiber and vitamin C

Good source of calcium and iron

Makes 3 cups oatmeal total

Serves 4 *(¾ cup oatmeal, ¾ cup berries, ¼ cup cream, and 2 Canadian bacon slices per serving)*

SERVE WITH

8 slices Canadian bacon (½ pound total), browned

Calories 90; total fat 4g (saturated fat 1.5g); protein 12g; carbohydrates 1g; fiber 0g; cholesterol 30mg; sodium 800mg; vitamin A 0%; vitamin C 0%; calcium 0%; iron 2%

On-the-Run Breakfast Cookies

with Fresh Apples and Cold Milk

Calories 350; total fat 7g (saturated fat 0.5g); protein 14g; carbohydrates 62g; fiber 7g; cholesterol 20mg; sodium 220mg; vitamin A 15%; vitamin C 15%; calcium 30%; iron 8%

4 cups high-protein, high-fiber cereal, such as Kashi GOLEAN Crunch!

½ cup quick-cooking oats

½ cup packed dark brown sugar

¾ teaspoon baking powder

½ teaspoon ground cinnamon

¼ cup canola oil

1 large egg plus 2 egg whites

⅔ cup dried cherries

▶ Preheat the oven to 350°F.

▶ Place the cereal in a food processor and process to a crumb texture. Add the remaining ingredients, except the cherries, and process until well blended. Remove the blade and stir in the cherries.

▶ Line a large cookie sheet with foil, and coat the foil with cooking spray. Spoon batter in ¼-cup amounts onto the cookie sheet, leaving a 2-inch space between the cookies. Bake 12 minutes or until slightly golden on edges. Do not overbake;

the cookies will not look totally done at this point, but they will continue to cook while cooling. Slide the foil (with the cookies on top) off the cookie sheet and let stand 7 minutes before removing the cookies.

▶ When they are completely cooled, store in an airtight container.

Calories 190; total fat 6g (saturated fat 0.5g); protein 5g; carbohydrates 29g; fiber 3g; cholesterol 20mg; sodium 90mg; vitamin A 6%; vitamin C 0%; calcium 2%; iron 6%

TIME-SHAVER TIP: *This is a perfect carpool breakfast. Just be sure to pack the apple and a container of milk for the road!*

Excellent source of fiber and calcium

Good source of vitamins A and C

Makes 12 cookies total

Serves 4 *(3 cookies, 1 apple, and 1 cup milk per serving)*

SERVE WITH

4 medium apples

Calories 70; total fat 0g (saturated fat 0g); protein 0g; carbohydrates 19g; fiber 3g; cholesterol 0mg; sodium 0mg; vitamin A 2%; vitamin C 10%; calcium 0%; iron 0%

4 cups fat-free milk

Calories 90; total fat 0g (saturated fat 0g); protein 9g; carbohydrates 13g; fiber 0g; cholesterol 5mg; sodium 130mg; vitamin A 10%; vitamin C 2%; calcium 25%; iron 0%

Hash Brown Casserole

with Grapefruit Halves and Chilled Tomato Juice

Calories 350; total fat 2g (saturated fat 0.5g); protein 16g; carbohydrates 66g; fiber 11g; cholesterol 25mg; sodium 760mg; vitamin A 60%; vitamin C 230%; calcium 10%; iron 10%

10 ounces smoked turkey sausage, diced

1½ medium onions, chopped (1½ cups)

½ 8-ounce package whole mushrooms, quartered

1 1-pound, 4-ounce package refrigerated diced potatoes with onions

¼ cup chopped parsley

▶ Place a large nonstick skillet over medium-high heat until hot. Coat the skillet with cooking spray, and cook the sausage 3 minutes or until beginning to brown, stirring frequently. Remove from the skillet and set aside on a separate plate.

▶ Recoat the skillet with cooking spray. Add the onion, coat with cooking spray, and cook 2 minutes; add the mushrooms and cook 3 minutes. Reduce the heat to medium, add the potatoes, and cook 9 minutes or until beginning to brown lightly. Remove from heat. Add the sausage and parsley, cover, and let stand 3 minutes to absorb flavors.

Calories 240; total fat 2g (saturated fat 0.5g); protein 14g; carbohydrates 40g; fiber 3g; cholesterol 25mg; sodium 620mg; vitamin A 6%; vitamin C 30%; calcium 4%; iron 8%

Excellent source of fiber and vitamins A and C

Good source of calcium and iron

Makes 4 cups casserole total

Serves 4 *(1 cup casserole, ½ grapefruit, and 1 cup juice per serving)*

SERVE WITH

2 medium grapefruit, halved

Calories 60; total fat 0g (saturated fat 0g); protein 1g; carbohydrates 16g; fiber 6g; cholesterol 0mg; sodium 0mg; vitamin A 15%; vitamin C 110%; calcium 2%; iron 0%

4 cups low-sodium tomato or vegetable juice

Calories 45; total fat 0g (saturated fat 0g); protein 1g; carbohydrates 10g; fiber 2g; cholesterol 0mg; sodium 130mg; vitamin A 35%; vitamin C 90%; calcium 4%; iron 4%

Broiled Breakfast Tomatoes

with Vegetable Link Sausage, Creamy Grits, and Mixed Citrus

Calories 350; total fat 10g (saturated fat 4.5g); protein 22g; carbohydrates 48g; fiber 8g; cholesterol 20mg; sodium 860mg; vitamin A 50%; vitamin C 170%; calcium 30%; iron 20%

2 large tomatoes, halved crosswise (14 ounces)

1 tablespoon plus 1 teaspoon dijonnaise

1 cup (4 ounces) finely shredded mozzarella cheese

2 slices reduced-calorie whole-wheat bread, toasted and grated

1 tablespoon plus 1 teaspoon grated Parmesan cheese

► Preheat the broiler.

► Arrange the tomato halves on a foil-lined baking pan. Spread 1 teaspoon of the dijonnaise evenly over each tomato half.

► Combine the mozzarella and bread crumbs in a medium bowl, and toss gently yet thoroughly to blend. Mound an equal amount on each tomato half, pressing down firmly to make it adhere.

► Broil no closer than 4 inches from the heat source for 1 minute. Turn off the broiler, tent with a sheet of foil, and let stand 8 minutes or until tomatoes are tender. Remove from the broiler, and sprinkle evenly with the Parmesan cheese. Serve hot or at room temperature.

Calories 130; total fat 7g (saturated fat 4g); protein 10g; carbohydrates 10g; fiber 3g; cholesterol 15mg; sodium 340mg; vitamin A 25%; vitamin C 25%; calcium 25%; iron 4%

TIME-SHAVER TIP: *Tear the toasted bread into small pieces and grate in a blender to a fine texture.*

Excellent source of fiber, vitamins A and C, calcium, and iron

Makes 4 tomato halves total

Serves 4 *(1 tomato half, 2 sausage links, ½ cup grits, ½ teaspoon margarine, and 1 cup fruit per serving)*

SERVE WITH

8 vegetarian sausage links, browned

    Calories 60; total fat 2g (saturated fat 0g); protein 9g; carbohydrates 2g; fiber 1g; cholesterol 0mg; sodium 360mg; vitamin A 0%; vitamin C 0%; calcium 0%; iron 10%

2 cups cooked grits, seasoned with ¼ teaspoon salt and topped with 2 teaspoons diet margarine

    Calories 80; total fat 1g (saturated fat 0g); protein 2g; carbohydrates 16g; fiber 0g; cholesterol 0mg; sodium 160mg; vitamin A 2%; vitamin C 0%; calcium 0%; iron 4%

4 cups mixed grapefruit and orange sections

    Calories 80; total fat 0g (saturated fat 0g); protein 2g; carbohydrates 20g; fiber 3g; cholesterol 0mg; sodium 0mg; vitamin A 25%; vitamin C 150%; calcium 4%; iron 2%

Apple Halvers

with Vegetable Breakfast Patties and Honey-Drizzled English Muffins

Calories 350; total fat 9g (saturated fat 1.5g); protein 23g; carbohydrates 47g; fiber 9g; cholesterol 0mg; sodium 700mg; vitamin A 8%; vitamin C 8%; calcium 6%; iron 25%

2 tablespoons plus 2 teaspoons diet margarine

1 tablespoon plus 1 teaspoon packed dark brown sugar

½ teaspoon vanilla extract

2 large Fuji or Gala apples (about 1 pound total), halved and cored

▶ Combine the margarine, sugar, and vanilla in a small bowl, and stir until well blended.

▶ Pierce the skin of each apple half in several areas with a fork. Place each apple half in a 6-ounce custard baking dish, cut side up; cover with plastic wrap and microwave on High 2 minutes or until just tender. Top each with equal amounts of the sugar mixture.

Calories 100; total fat 3g (saturated fat 0.5g); protein 0g; carbohydrates 21g; fiber 3g; cholesterol 0mg; sodium 65mg; vitamin A 8%; vitamin C 8%; calcium 2%; iron 2%

TIME-SHAVER TIP: *Piercing the skin of the apple allows steam to escape, which allows it to cook faster.*

Excellent source of fiber and iron

Makes 4 apple halves total

Serves 4 (*1 apple half, 2 sausage patties, ½ muffin, and 1 teaspoon honey per serving*)

SERVE WITH

8 vegetable breakfast sausage patties, browned

Calories 160; total fat 6g (saturated fat 1g); protein 20g; carbohydrates 7g; fiber 4g; cholesterol 0mg; sodium 520mg; vitamin A 0%; vitamin C 0%; calcium 4%; iron 20%

2 whole-wheat English muffins, split, toasted, and drizzled with 1 tablespoon plus 1 teaspoon honey

Calories 90; total fat 1g (saturated fat 0g); protein 3g; carbohydrates 19g; fiber 2g; cholesterol 0mg; sodium 120mg; vitamin A 0%; vitamin C 0%; calcium 2%; iron 4%

Big-Bowl Cereal Parfait

with Toasted Buttery Raisin Bagels

Calories 350; total fat 9g (saturated fat 1g); protein 15g; carbohydrates 58g; fiber 7g; cholesterol 5mg; sodium 310mg; vitamin A 8%; vitamin C 160%; calcium 40%; iron 20%

4 cups whole strawberries, quartered

3 tablespoons pourable sugar substitute, such as Splenda

1 cup cereal, such as Special K or Fiber One

⅓ cup (1½ ounces) sliced almonds, toasted

2 tablespoons wheat germ

1 to 2 teaspoons grated lemon rind

4 6-ounce containers fat-free vanilla yogurt sweetened with aspartame (3 cups total)

▶ Combine the strawberries and sugar substitute in a medium bowl.

▶ Combine the remaining ingredients, except the yogurt, in a small bowl, and toss gently yet thoroughly until well blended.

▶ Spoon the yogurt into four shallow soup bowls, top with equal amounts of the berries and sprinkle the cereal mixture on top of each.

Calories 250; total fat 7g (saturated fat 0.5g); protein 11g; carbohydrates 37g; fiber 5g; cholesterol 5mg; sodium 160mg; vitamin A 4%; vitamin C 160%; calcium 30%; iron 20%

COOK'S NOTE: The addition of grated lemon rind gives a very refreshing taste to the parfait. Don't underestimate the power of the rind.

Excellent source of fiber, vitamin C, calcium, and iron

Makes 3 cups yogurt, 4 cups strawberries, and 1⅓ cups cereal mixture total

Serves 4 *(¾ cup yogurt, 1 cup strawberries, ⅓ cup cereal mixture, ½ bagel, and 1 teaspoon margarine per serving)*

SERVE WITH

2 raisin bagels, halved and toasted, and 4 teaspoons diet margarine

Calories 100; total fat 2g (saturated fat 0g); protein 4g; carbohydrates 20g; fiber 3g; cholesterol 0mg; sodium 150mg; vitamin A 4%; vitamin C 0%; calcium 10%; iron 4%

Tropical Fruit and Yogurt Platters

with Canadian Bacon and Whole-Wheat Toast

Calories 320; total fat 4.5g (saturated fat 1.5g); protein 21g; carbohydrates 57g; fiber 7g; cholesterol 30mg; sodium 1,020mg; vitamin A 2%; vitamin C 120%; calcium 42%; iron 8%

4 6-ounce containers light lemon chiffon or piña colada yogurt sweetened with aspartame (3 cups total)

2 cups diced fresh pineapple

2 ripe kiwi, peeled and sliced (1 cup)

1 medium banana, peeled and sliced (1 cup)

4 medium lemons

4 teaspoons sugar

▶ Spoon 1 container of yogurt into the center of four individual bread or dessert plates. Decoratively arrange equal amounts of the pineapple, kiwi, and banana slices around the yogurt.

▶ Grate 2 teaspoons of the lemon rind and sprinkle evenly over the fruit. In a small bowl, combine the juice from the lemons with the sugar and stir until well blended. Spoon evenly over each serving of fruit.

Calories 220; total fat 0g (saturated fat 0g); protein 9g; carbohydrates 47g; fiber 3g; cholesterol 5mg; sodium 130mg; vitamin A 2%; vitamin C 120%; calcium 40%; iron 2%

COOK'S NOTE: *The juices from the lemon and fruits will run into the yogurt, adding even more flavor to the dish.*

Excellent source of fiber, vitamin C, and calcium

Makes 3 cups yogurt plus about 4 cups fruit total

Serves 4 *(¾ cup yogurt, 1 cup fruit, 2 Canadian bacon slices, and 1 slice toast per serving)*

SERVE WITH

8 slices Canadian bacon (½ pound total), browned

Calories 90; total fat 4g (saturated fat 1.5g); protein 12g; carbohydrates 1g; fiber 0g; cholesterol 30mg; sodium 800mg; vitamin A 0%; vitamin C 0%; calcium 0%; iron 2%

4 slices reduced-calorie whole-wheat bread, toasted

Calories 40; total fat 0g (saturated fat 0g); protein 2g; carbohydrates 9g; fiber 4g; cholesterol 0mg; sodium 120mg; vitamin A 0%; vitamin C 0%; calcium 2%; iron 4%

Peach-Pineapple Breakfast Drink

with Peanut Buttery Toast

Calories 350; total fat 10g (saturated fat 1.5g); protein 16g; carbohydrates 52g; fiber 6g; cholesterol 0mg; sodium 390mg; vitamin A 20%; vitamin C 15%; calcium 40%; iron 15%

2½ cups light vanilla soy milk

6 ounces (about 1¼ cups) frozen unsweetened peaches

½ 8-ounce can crushed pineapple in juice, undrained

¼ cup apricot fruit spread

½ teaspoon vanilla extract

▶ Combine all the ingredients in a blender, secure the lid, and puree until smooth.

Calories 220; total fat 1.5g (saturated fat 0g); protein 10g; carbohydrates 40g; fiber 2g; cholesterol 0mg; sodium 240mg; vitamin A 20%; vitamin C 15%; calcium 40%; iron 6%

COOK'S NOTE: *Replace the peaches with mangoes and the vanilla with ¼ teaspoon coconut extract for a more tropical flavor, if desired.*

Excellent source of fiber, vitamin A, and calcium

Good source of vitamin C and iron

Makes 4 cups peach mixture total

Serves 2 *(2 cups peach mixture, 1 slice toast, and 1 tablespoon peanut butter per serving)*

SERVE WITH

2 slices reduced-calorie whole-wheat bread, toasted, and 2 tablespoons reduced-fat creamy or crunchy peanut butter

Calories 140; total fat 8g (saturated fat 1.5g); protein 6g; carbohydrates 12g; fiber 5g; cholesterol 0mg; sodium 150mg; vitamin A 0%; vitamin C 0%; calcium 2%; iron 6%

Travel Mug Breakfast

Calories 350; total fat 11g (saturated fat 2.5g); protein 17g; carbohydrates 46g; fiber 4g; cholesterol 0mg; sodium 470mg; vitamin A 15%; vitamin C 8%; calcium 45%; iron 15%

3 cups light chocolate soy milk

1 medium banana, peeled

1 tablespoon instant coffee granules

3 tablespoons creamy reduced-fat peanut butter

5 to 6 ice cubes, optional

> **Makes 4 cups beverage total**
>
> **Serves 2** *(2 cups beverage per serving)*

▶ Combine all the ingredients in a blender, secure the lid, and puree until smooth.

TIME-SHAVER TIP: You may blend the mixture together and refrigerate overnight. Stir or puree again before serving.

Excellent source of calcium

Good source of fiber, vitamin A, and iron

Snacks and Appetizers

CRUNCHY SNACKS

- ▸ Southwestern Chex Crunch
- ▸ Tangy Dill Pita Chips
- ▸ Sweet and Crunchy Snack Mix
- ▸ Sweet and Sticky Cinnamon Popcorn Balls
- ▸ Crunchy, Nutty Cereal Mounds
- ▸ Graham Cracker Stacks

DIPS, SALSAS, AND SPREADS

- ▸ Fresh Lime and Avocado Dip
- ▸ Refried Bean and Avocado Stacker Dip
- ▸ Creamy, Cheesy, Spicy Spinach
- ▸ Shrimp with Fresh Lemon Aioli
- ▸ Creamy Pumpkin Pie Dip
- ▸ Citrus Cream
- ▸ Creamy, Peanutty, Chocolatey Dip
- ▸ Crunchy Fruit Citrus Dip
- ▸ Black Bean and Mozzarella Simple Salsa
- ▸ Red Pepper and White Bean Toss

- ▸ Tomato-Peperoncini on Crostini
- ▸ Mexican Black Bean Hummus
- ▸ Roasted Pepper and Kalamata Hummus
- ▸ Two-Cheese Pimiento Topper
- ▸ Creamy Cream Cheese with Raspberry Pepper Jelly

PICKUPS

- ▸ Sherried Garlic Mushrooms
- ▸ Mini Potato Bakers
- ▸ Pepperoni Bites
- ▸ Jalapeño Melts
- ▸ Pizza Pinchers
- ▸ Antipasto Skewers
- ▸ Salmon-Topped Cucumber Rounds
- ▸ Cheese Bundles
- ▸ Double-Stuffed Deviled Eggs

Southwestern Chex Crunch

Calories 130; total fat 6g (saturated fat 1g); protein 3g; carbohydrates 22g; fiber 2g; cholesterol 0mg; sodium 400mg; vitamin A 4%; vitamin C 4%; calcium 4%; iron 30%

4 cups whole-grain or multigrain Chex cereal

1 cup (2 ounces) low-sodium cheese-flavored fish crackers, such as Pepperidge Farm Goldfish

2 cups (2 ounces) toasted garlic bagel chips, broken in fourths

1 tablespoon Worcestershire sauce

1 tablespoon prepared mustard

2 teaspoons canola oil

½ 1.25-ounce packet 40% less-sodium taco seasoning mix

> Makes 6 cups snack mix total
>
> Serves 8 (about ¾ cup snack mix per serving)

▶ Preheat the oven to 300°F.

▶ Combine the cereal, crackers, and bagel pieces in a large bowl and set aside.

▶ Combine the Worcestershire sauce, mustard, and oil in a small bowl, and stir until well blended. Spoon over the cereal mixture and toss gently yet thoroughly to coat completely. Sprinkle the seasoning mix evenly over all and toss until well coated. Place on a large baking sheet in a single layer and bake 11 to 12 minutes or until beginning to brown lightly.

▶ Remove the pan from the oven, place on a wire rack, and let stand 2 hours. Store leftovers in an airtight container in a dry pantry.

TIME-SHAVER TIP: For an easy "grab-and-go" snack, package servings in individual plastic ziptop bags.

Excellent source of iron

Tangy Dill Pita Chips

Calories 130; total fat 1g (saturated fat 0g); protein 3g; carbohydrates 18g; fiber 2g; cholesterol 0mg; sodium 420mg; vitamin A 2%; vitamin C 0%; calcium 6%; iron 6%

Makes 48 wedges total

Serves 6 (*8 wedges per serving*)

4 whole-wheat pita breads, cut in half crosswise (making 8 rounds)

½ 1-ounce packet dry ranch salad dressing mix

1 teaspoon dried dill weed

▶ Preheat the oven to 350°F.

▶ Place the pita rounds on a cutting board, smooth side down, and coat lightly with cooking spray. Sprinkle evenly with the salad dressing mix and dill. Cut each round into six wedges and arrange on two cookie sheets.

▶ Bake 6 to 7 minutes or until lightly golden on edges. Place on a rack to cool completely. Store in an airtight container.

COOK'S NOTE: *You can serve these as a snack or with a salad for an interesting accompaniment.*

Sweet and Crunchy Snack Mix

Calories 150; total fat 5g (saturated fat 0.5g); protein 6g; carbohydrates 22g; fiber 4g; cholesterol 0mg; sodium 140mg; vitamin A 6%; vitamin C 0%; calcium 2%; iron 6%

Makes 2 cups snack mix total

Serves 4 (½ *cup snack mix per serving*)

1½ cups crunchy high-fiber cereal, such as Kashi GOLEAN Crunch!

¼ cup dried cherries

¼ cup (1 ounce) dry-roasted peanuts, salted variety, if desired

▶ Combine all ingredients in a medium bowl and toss to blend well.

COOK'S NOTE: *To bring out the nutty flavor of the peanuts, toast and cool them before adding to the other ingredients. To toast nuts, heat a skillet over medium-high heat until hot; add the nuts and cook 2 to 3 minutes or until fragrant and beginning to brown lightly, stirring frequently.*

Good source of fiber

Sweet and Sticky Cinnamon Popcorn Balls

Calories 150; total fat 4.5g (saturated fat 0g); protein 3g; carbohydrates 28g; fiber 2g; cholesterol 0mg; sodium 140mg; vitamin A 0%; vitamin C 0%; calcium 2%; iron 2%

1 2.9-ounce packet 94% fat-free microwave popcorn

½ cup (2 ounces) slivered almonds

½ cup light or dark corn syrup

½ teaspoon ground cinnamon

Makes 14 popcorn balls total

Serves 7 *(2 popcorn balls per serving)*

▶ Place the popcorn in the microwave and cook according to the directions on the package.

▶ Meanwhile, place a small skillet over medium-high heat until hot. Add the almonds and cook 2 to 3 minutes or until golden, stirring constantly. Remove from the skillet and set aside on a separate plate. Add the corn syrup to the skillet and bring to a boil.

▶ Place the popcorn on a large cookie sheet, discarding any unpopped kernels. Sprinkle evenly with the cinnamon and almonds. Pour the corn syrup over the popcorn and toss until well coated.

▶ Form into 14 balls. If the mixture is too sticky to mold, spread in a thin layer on the cookie sheet and let stand 30 minutes to dry slightly. Store popcorn balls in single layers between sheets of waxed paper in an airtight container.

COOK'S NOTE: *For easier handling, spray your fingertips with cooking spray while forming the balls.*

Crunchy, Nutty Cereal Mounds

Calories 150; total fat 7g (saturated fat 1g); protein 5g; carbohydrates 23g; fiber 4g; cholesterol 0mg; sodium 80mg; vitamin A 2%; vitamin C 0%; calcium 2%; iron 6%

Makes 12 mounds total

Serves 12 *(1 mound per serving)*

½ cup (2 ounces) pecan pieces

3 tablespoons margarine (not diet margarine)

1½ cups mini marshmallows

¼ cup light corn syrup

4 cups high-fiber cereal, such as Kashi GOLEAN Crunch!

▶ Preheat the oven to 350°F.

▶ Coat a 12-cup nonstick muffin tin with cooking spray and set aside.

▶ Heat a large saucepan over medium heat until hot. Add the pecans and cook 3 minutes, stirring constantly, until they begin to brown lightly and are fragrant. Reduce heat to low, and add the margarine. When the margarine is melted, add the marshmallows and corn syrup; stir until the marshmallows are completely melted. Add the cereal and stir to coat.

▶ Working quickly, mound equal amounts of the cereal mixture in each of the 12 muffin cups. Press each with your fingertips to form a rounded mound and let stand 5 minutes.

▶ Serve immediately for sticky mounds or let stand 1 hour for crunchier mounds. Store in an airtight container.

COOK'S NOTE: *This snack needs to be assembled very quickly, so be sure to have all the ingredients ready before beginning.*

Good source of fiber

Graham Cracker Stacks

Calories 150; total fat 3.5g (saturated fat 0.5g); protein 3g; carbohydrates 28g; fiber 2g; cholesterol 0mg; sodium 105mg; vitamin A 0%; vitamin C 8%; calcium 0%; iron 4%

Makes 8 stacks total

Serves 4 (2 stacks per serving)

⅓ cup fat-free whipped topping

1½ tablespoons reduced-fat creamy or chunky peanut butter

8 low-fat graham cracker squares, 2½-inch squares each

2 small bananas, peeled and sliced (1⅓ cups)

⅛ teaspoon ground nutmeg

▶ In a small bowl, combine the whipped topping and peanut butter; stir until well blended. Spread equal amounts (about 1 tablespoon) on each of the graham crackers, top with banana slices, and sprinkle with the nutmeg.

TIME-SHAVER TIP: For easier blending, microwave the peanut butter on High for 20 to 30 seconds to soften slightly.

Fresh Lime and Avocado Dip

with Corn Tortilla Wedges

Calories 140; total fat 4.5g (saturated fat 1g); protein 5g; carbohydrates 23g; fiber 4g; cholesterol 0mg; sodium 350mg; vitamin A 4%; vitamin C 6%; calcium 8%; iron 4%

1 medium ripe avocado, peeled and seeded

½ 15.5-ounce can navy beans, rinsed and drained

¾ cup fat-free sour cream

2 tablespoons lime juice

½ 0.7-ounce packet dry Italian salad dressing mix

▶ Combine all ingredients in a blender or food processor and puree until smooth.

Calories 90; total fat 3.5g (saturated fat 0.5g); protein 3g; carbohydrates 11g; fiber 2g; cholesterol 0mg; sodium 340mg; vitamin A 4%; vitamin C 6%; calcium 6%; iron 2%

COOK'S NOTE: To store, cover the dip with plastic wrap and refrigerate up to 3 days. Place chips in an airtight container in the pantry.

Good source of fiber

Makes 1¾ cups dip total

Serves 7 (¼ cup dip and 8 tortilla wedges per serving)

SERVE WITH

7 soft soft corn tortillas, cut into 8 wedges each, baked in a 350°F oven for 8 minutes, and cooled completely

Calories 60; total fat 0.5g (saturated fat 0g); protein 1g; carbohydrates 12g; fiber 2g; cholesterol 0mg; sodium 10mg; vitamin A 0%; vitamin C 0%; calcium 2%; iron 2%

Refried Bean and Avocado Stacker Dip

with Corn Tortilla Wedges

Calories 150; total fat 3.5g (saturated fat 0.5 g); protein 5g; carbohydrates 24g; fiber 5g; cholesterol 5mg; sodium 300mg; vitamin A 6%; vitamin C 10%; calcium 8%; iron 8%

1 16-ounce can fat-free refried beans

1½ medium limes

1 teaspoon ground cumin

1½ cups (12 ounces) fat-free sour cream

1 4-ounce can chopped mild green chilies, drained

1 medium tomato, seeded and chopped (1 cup)

24 small pitted ripe olives, sliced

1 medium ripe avocado, peeled, seeded, and chopped
   (1 cup)

▶ Combine the beans, juice of one lime, and cumin in a bowl, and stir until well blended. Spoon into the bottom of a 9-inch deep-dish pie pan or casserole dish. Spoon sour cream over all, using the back of a spoon to spread evenly. Top with, in order, the chilies, tomato, olives, and avocado.

▶ Cut the remaining lime half in half again and squeeze the juice evenly over the avocado. Serve with chips.

Calories 90; total fat 3g (saturated fat 0.5g); protein 4g; carbohydrates 12g; fiber 3g; cholesterol 5mg; sodium 290mg; vitamin A 6%; vitamin C 10%; calcium 6%; iron 6%

COOK'S NOTE: Be sure to drain the green chilies. There may not be a large amount of liquid, but if it's not drained, it may water down the other layers.

Good source of fiber and vitamin C

Makes 4 cups dip total

Serves 12 (⅓ cup dip and 8 tortilla wedges per serving)

SERVE WITH

12 soft soft corn tortillas, cut into 8 wedges each and baked in a 350°F oven for 8 minutes

Calories 60; total fat 0.5g (saturated fat 0g); protein 1g; carbohydrates 12g; fiber 2g; cholesterol 0mg; sodium 10mg; vitamin A 0%; vitamin C 0%; calcium 2%; iron 2%

Creamy, Cheesy, Spicy Spinach

with Garlic Melba Rounds

Calories 150; total fat 4.5g (saturated fat 2.5g); protein 7g; carbohydrates 18g; fiber 2g; cholesterol 20mg; sodium 450mg; vitamin A 60%; vitamin C 15%; calcium 25%; iron 8%

½ medium yellow onion, chopped (½ cup)

1 10-ounce package frozen chopped spinach, thawed and squeezed dry

¾ cup fat-free milk

¾ cup (3 ounces) reduced-fat sharp cheddar cheese, shredded (or reduced-fat American cheese slices, torn in small pieces)

6 tablespoons (3 ounces) light cream cheese, tub style

2 teaspoons Worcestershire sauce

⅛ teaspoon cayenne pepper

▶ Place a 12-inch nonstick skillet over medium-high heat until hot. Coat the skillet with cooking spray, add the onion, and cook 3 minutes or until translucent, stirring frequently. Reduce heat to medium; add the spinach and milk, and cook 1 minute or until the liquid is almost evaporated. Add the remaining ingredients, and cook 1 minute or until well blended, stirring constantly.

▶ Remove from heat; let stand 5 minutes to absorb flavors and thicken slightly before serving.

Calories 80; total fat 4g (saturated fat 2.5g); protein 5g; carbohydrates 4g; fiber 1g; cholesterol 20mg; sodium 300mg; vitamin A 60%; vitamin C 15%; calcium 20%; iron 4%

TIME-SHAVER TIP: *To thaw spinach fast, place it in a shallow pan in the microwave on High for 4 to 5 minutes.*

Excellent source of vitamin A and calcium

Good source of vitamin C

Makes 2 cups spinach mixture total

Serves 8 *(¼ cup spinach mixture and 6 melba rounds per serving)*

SERVE WITH

48 garlic-flavored melba rounds

Calories 70; total fat 0.5g (saturated fat 0g); protein 2g; carbohydrates 14g; fiber 1g; cholesterol 0mg; sodium 150mg; vitamin A 0%; vitamin C 0%; calcium 2%; iron 4%

Shrimp with Fresh Lemon Aioli

Calories 150; total fat 4g (saturated fat 0g); protein 23g; carbohydrates 4g; fiber 0g; cholesterol 210mg; sodium 460mg; vitamin A 6%; vitamin C 10%; calcium 6%; iron 20%

4 cups water

1 tablespoon liquid shrimp and crab boil or to taste, such as Zatarain's

1¼ pounds raw headless medium shrimp, unpeeled

¼ cup fat-free sour cream

2 tablespoons light mayonnaise

2 medium garlic cloves, minced

1 teaspoon grated lemon rind

1½ to 2 tablespoons lemon juice

Louisiana hot sauce to taste

¼ teaspoon salt

Makes about 15 ounces cooked shrimp and ½ cup sauce total

Serves 4 (about 3 ounces cooked shrimp and 2 tablespoons sauce per serving)

▶ Bring the water and shrimp and crab boil to a boil in a Dutch oven over high heat. Add the shrimp, return to a boil, and cook 2 minutes or until the shrimp are opaque in the center. Remove from heat and let stand 2 minutes to absorb flavors. Drain well and place on a sheet of foil or large cookie sheet in a single layer to cool quickly, about 10 minutes.

▶ Meanwhile, combine the remaining ingredients in a small bowl and stir until well blended. Cover with plastic wrap and refrigerate until needed.

▶ When the shrimp have cooled, peel but leave the tails attached. Refrigerate until serving time. Place them on a lettuce-lined platter, if desired, and serve with the aioli.

COOK'S NOTE: *Anytime you want to s-t-r-e-t-c-h your mayonnaise flavor and texture without adding more fat to your dish, substitute fat-free sour cream for half the mayonnaise.*

Excellent source of iron

Good source of vitamin C

Creamy Pumpkin Pie Dip

with Sliced Apples

Calories 150; total fat 2g (saturated fat 1g); protein 2g; carbohydrates 29g; fiber 4g; cholesterol 5mg; sodium 120mg; vitamin A 110%; vitamin C 10%; calcium 2%; iron 4%

½ 15-ounce can solid pumpkin

6 tablespoons (3 ounces) light cream cheese, tub style

3 tablespoons pourable sugar substitute, such as Splenda, or sugar

1 teaspoon ground cinnamon

⅛ teaspoon ground nutmeg

¼ teaspoon vanilla, butter, and nut flavoring or ½ teaspoon vanilla extract

1 8-ounce container fat-free whipped topping

▶ Combine the pumpkin; cream cheese; sugar; cinnamon; nutmeg; and vanilla, butter, and nut flavoring in a medium bowl. Stir until well blended. Add the whipped topping and stir until just blended. Serve immediately or cover with plastic wrap and store in the refrigerator until serving time.

Calories 80; total fat 1.5g (saturated fat 1g); protein 1g; carbohydrates 10g; fiber 1g; cholesterol 5mg; sodium 115mg; vitamin A 110%; vitamin C 2%; calcium 2%; iron 2%

COOK'S NOTE: *If apple slices are cut in advance, be sure to squeeze a bit of lemon or orange juice over them and cover with plastic wrap to prevent discoloration.*

Excellent source of vitamin A

Good source of fiber and vitamin C

Makes 3 cups dip total

Serves 9 *(⅓ cup dip and about 1 cup fruit slices per serving)*

SERVE WITH

9 medium apples, sliced (about 9 cups)

Calories 70; total fat 0g (saturated fat 0g); protein 0g; carbohydrates 19g; fiber 3g; cholesterol 0mg; sodium 0mg; vitamin A 2%; vitamin C 10%; calcium 0%; iron 0%

Citrus Cream

with Sliced Bananas

Calories 150; total fat 2g (saturated fat 1.5g); protein 2g; carbohydrates 32g; fiber 3g; cholesterol 5mg; sodium 20mg; vitamin A 4%; vitamin C 20%; calcium 6%; iron 2%

1 6-ounce container low-fat vanilla yogurt

¾ cup fat-free whipped topping

1 teaspoon grated lemon rind

1 tablespoon lemon juice

½ teaspoon grated orange zest

1 tablespoon sugar

½ teaspoon vanilla extract

▶ Combine all the ingredients in a small bowl and stir until well blended.

Calories 60; total fat 1.5g (saturated fat 1.5g); protein 1g; carbohydrates 9g; fiber 0g; cholesterol 5mg; sodium 15mg; vitamin A 2%; vitamin C 2%; calcium 6%; iron 0%

Makes 1½ cups sauce total

Serves 6 (¼ cup sauce, ⅔ cup sliced bananas, and 2 teaspoons orange juice per serving)

SERVE WITH

4 medium bananas, peeled, sliced (4 cups), and tossed with ¼ cup orange juice and served with toothpicks

Calories 90; total fat 0g (saturated fat 0g); protein 1g; carbohydrates 23g; fiber 3g; cholesterol 0mg; sodium 0mg; vitamin A 2%; vitamin C 20%; calcium 0%; iron 2%

TIME-SHAVER TIP: *To grate items in a flash—from citrus and ginger to garlic and hard cheese—pick up a microplane grater (a fine grater) wherever kitchen gadgets are sold. Buy the variety with a rubber handle for easier use.*

COOK'S NOTE: *The orange juice will prevent the bananas from discoloring.*

Excellent source of vitamin C

Good source of fiber

Creamy, Peanutty, Chocolatey Dip

with Sliced Apples

Calories 150; total fat 3g (saturated fat 0.5g); protein 3g; carbohydrates 28g; fiber 3g; cholesterol 0mg; sodium 240mg; vitamin A 2%; vitamin C 8%; calcium 4%; iron 4%

Makes about 2 cups dip total

Serves 6 *(¼ cup dip and 1 cup sliced apples per serving)*

¾ **to 1 cup fat-free milk**

1 1-ounce package sugar-free, fat-free instant chocolate pudding mix

¼ **cup reduced-fat creamy peanut butter**

½ **8-ounce container fat-free whipped topping**

▶ Whisk together the milk and pudding mix in a medium bowl until well blended.

▶ Place the peanut butter in a microwave-safe bowl, and microwave on High for 30 seconds or until slightly melted. Whisk the peanut butter into the pudding mixture until well blended, and fold in the whipped topping.

Calories 100; total fat 3g (saturated fat 0.5g); protein 3g; carbohydrates 14g; fiber 1g; cholesterol 0mg; sodium 240mg; vitamin A 0%; vitamin C 0%; calcium 4%; iron 4%

SERVE WITH

6 medium apples, sliced (about 6 cups)

Calories 50; total fat 0g (saturated fat 0g); protein 0g; carbohydrates 14g; fiber 2g; cholesterol 0mg; sodium 0mg; vitamin A 2%; vitamin C 8%; calcium 0%; iron 0%

COOK'S NOTE: *Don't skip the microwave step for the peanut butter; it makes it easier to blend with the other ingredients.*

Good source of fiber

Crunchy Fruit Citrus Dip

with Crisp Pear Slices

Calories 140; total fat 0g (saturated fat 0g); protein 1g; carbohydrates 39g; fiber 6g; cholesterol 0mg; sodium 0mg; vitamin A 4%; vitamin C 15%; calcium 2%; iron 2%

½ cup pourable sugar substitute, such as Splenda

2 teaspoons grated lemon rind

½ cup lemon juice

¼ cup orange juice

▶ In a medium bowl, combine all the ingredients and stir until well blended. Pour into four small bowls.

Calories 25; total fat 0g (saturated fat 0g); protein 0g; carbohydrates 7g; fiber 0g; cholesterol 0mg; sodium 0mg; vitamin A 0%; vitamin C 0%; calcium 0%; iron 0%

TIME-SHAVER TIP: *Have a reamer? If not, pick one up wherever kitchen gadgets are sold. This inexpensive, indispensable kitchen tool resembles a large, ridged teardrop with a handle and is generally made of wood. Use it for juicing any variety of citrus fruit easily.*

Excellent source of fiber

Good source of vitamin C

Makes ½ cup dipping sauce total

Serves 4 *(2 tablespoons sauce and 1¼ cups pear slices per serving)*

SERVE WITH

4 large firm pears, sliced (about 5 cups)

Calories 110; total fat 0g (saturated fat 0g); protein 1g; carbohydrates 29g; fiber 5g; cholesterol 0mg; sodium 0mg; vitamin A 2%; vitamin C 15%; calcium 2%; iron 2%

Black Bean and Mozzarella Simple Salsa

with Corn Tortilla Wedges

Calories 150; total fat 4.5g (saturated fat 2g); protein 7g; carbohydrates 23g; fiber 4g; cholesterol 5mg; sodium 330mg; vitamin A 6%; vitamin C 8%; calcium 15%; iron 6%

1 10-ounce can diced tomatoes with green chilies, drained

½ 15-ounce can black beans, rinsed and drained

½ medium cucumber, peeled and diced (1 cup)

¼ cup finely chopped onion

1 cup (4 ounces) mozzarella cheese, chopped fine (about ¼-inch cubes)

3 to 4 tablespoons chopped cilantro

1 tablespoon lime juice

▶ Combine all the ingredients in a medium bowl and toss gently yet thoroughly to blend. Cover with plastic wrap and let stand 1 hour to absorb flavors.

Calories 70; total fat 3g (saturated fat 2g); protein 5g; carbohydrates 5g; fiber 2g; cholesterol 5mg; sodium 310mg; vitamin A 6%; vitamin C 8%; calcium 10%; iron 4%

TIME-SHAVER TIP: No time to chop the cheese? Pick up the reduced-fat cheese "crumbles" in the dairy section of your supermarket instead.

Good source of fiber and calcium

Makes about 3 cups salsa total

Serves 8 (about ⅓ cup salsa and 9 chips per serving)

SERVE WITH

12 soft soft corn tortillas, cut into 6 wedges each, baked in a 350°F oven for 8 minutes, and cooled completely

Calories 90; total fat 1g (saturated fat 0g); protein 2g; carbohydrates 17g; fiber 2g; cholesterol 0mg; sodium 20mg; vitamin A 0%; vitamin C 0%; calcium 4%; iron 2%

Red Pepper and White Bean Toss

with Crisp, Fresh Garlic Toast

Calories 140; total fat 2.5g (saturated fat 0.5g); protein 5g; carbohydrates 23g; fiber 2g; cholesterol 0mg; sodium 480mg; vitamin A 10%; vitamin C 8%; calcium 6%; iron 8%

1 12-ounce jar roasted red peppers, drained and chopped (or 1 cup chopped)

1½ medium tomatoes, seeded and chopped (1½ cups)

½ 15.5-ounce can navy beans, rinsed and drained

1 to 2 tablespoons capers, drained

2 tablespoons chopped basil leaves

1 tablespoon extra-virgin olive oil

1 medium garlic clove, minced

⅛ teaspoon dried pepper flakes

▶ Combine all the ingredients and toss gently yet thoroughly to blend.

Calories 70; total fat 2g (saturated fat 0g); protein 2g; carbohydrates 8g; fiber 1g; cholesterol 0mg; sodium 320mg; vitamin A 10%; vitamin C 8%; calcium 2%; iron 4%

COOK'S NOTE: *Why seed tomatoes? They hold a lot of water; when the seeds are removed, so is the watery portion of the tomato that can dilute the dish. To seed tomatoes easily, cut them in half crosswise, squeeze each half, and the seeds and membrane come out.*

Good source of vitamin A

Makes 2 cups pepper mixture total

Serves 8 *(¼ cup pepper mixture and 5 slices garlic toast per serving)*

SERVE WITH

8 ounces baguette bread, cut into ¼-inch slices (40 slices total), baked in a 350°F oven for 10 minutes, cooled completely, and rubbed with 2 halved medium garlic cloves

Calories 70; total fat 1g (saturated fat 0g); protein 2g; carbohydrates 15g; fiber 1g; cholesterol 0mg; sodium 150mg; vitamin A 0%; vitamin C 0%; calcium 4%; iron 4%

Tomato-Peperoncini on Crostini

Calories 150; total fat 6g (saturated fat 2g); protein 6g; carbohydrates 20g; fiber 2g; cholesterol 5mg; sodium 530mg; vitamin A 30%; vitamin C 50%; calcium 8%; iron 8%

Makes 24 crostini total

Serves 4 *(6 crostini per serving)*

4 ounces French bread (preferably baguette), cut into 24 thin slices

3 medium plum tomatoes, chopped fine (2 cups)

1 4-ounce container chopped pimiento, drained

8 small peperoncinis, chopped fine (about 2 ounces total)

1 tablespoon finely chopped fresh oregano, or 1 teaspoon dried oregano leaves

1 tablespoon extra-virgin olive oil

2 medium garlic cloves, halved crosswise

½ cup (2 ounces) reduced-fat crumbled feta

▶ Preheat the oven to 350°F.

▶ Arrange the bread slices in a single layer on a large cookie sheet, and bake 8 minutes or until just lightly golden. Remove from the oven and cool completely.

▶ Meanwhile, combine the tomatoes, pimiento, peperoncinis, oregano, and olive oil in a medium bowl, and stir gently yet thoroughly to blend.

▶ When the bread has cooled, gently rub the cut side of the garlic halves over the top of each bread slice. Spoon equal amounts of the tomato mixture on top of each slice and sprinkle with cheese.

COOK'S NOTE: *Don't skip the garlic-rubbing step. The garlic provides an entire layer of flavor.*

Excellent source of vitamins A and C

Mexican Black Bean Hummus

with Corn Tortilla Wedges

Calories 140; total fat 1.5g (saturated fat 0 g); protein 6g; carbohydrates 26g; fiber 7g; cholesterol 0mg; sodium 390mg; vitamin A 2%; vitamin C 2%; calcium 6%; iron 10%

½ 15-ounce can black beans, rinsed and drained

½ cup picante sauce

3 tablespoons lime juice

1 medium garlic clove, peeled

2 tablespoons chopped cilantro

½ teaspoon ground cumin

▶ Combine all the ingredients in a blender or small food processor, and puree until smooth.

Calories 70; total fat 0.5g (saturated fat 0 g); protein 4g; carbohydrates 11g; fiber 5g; cholesterol 0mg; sodium 370mg; vitamin A 2%; vitamin C 2%; calcium 2%; iron 8%

TIME-SHAVER TIP: *You can triple or quadruple the recipe for tortillas, cool completely, and then store them in an airtight container for weeks to have on hand! Go one step further and store servings in individual bags for easy, "portion-controlled" snacks.*

Excellent source of fiber

Good source of iron

Makes about 1 cup bean mixture total

Serves 4 (*about ¼ cup bean mixture and 10 chips per serving*)

SERVE WITH

5 soft soft corn tortillas, cut into 8 wedges each, baked in a 350°F oven for 8 minutes, and cooled completely.

Calories 70; total fat 1g (saturated fat 0g); protein 2g; carbohydrates 15g; fiber 2g; cholesterol 0mg; sodium 15mg; vitamin A 0%; vitamin C 0%; calcium 2%; iron 2%

59

Roasted Pepper and Kalamata Hummus

with Whole-Wheat Pita Chips

Calories 150; total fat 5g (saturated fat 0.5g); protein 5g; carbohydrates 23g; fiber 4g; cholesterol 0mg; sodium 420mg; vitamin A 4%; vitamin C 8%; calcium 2%; iron 8%

1 15.5-ounce can garbanzo beans, rinsed and drained

¼ cup (2 ounces) roasted red peppers

12 pitted kalamata olives

4 sun-dried tomato halves

¼ cup water

1 to 2 tablespoons lemon juice

1 tablespoon chopped fresh basil leaves

2 teaspoons extra-virgin olive oil

2 medium garlic cloves, peeled

¼ teaspoon salt

▶ Combine all the ingredients in a food processor and puree until smooth.

Calories 90; total fat 4.5g (saturated fat 0g); protein 3g; carbohydrates 11g; fiber 2g; cholesterol 0mg; sodium 300mg; vitamin A 4%; vitamin C 8%; calcium 2%; iron 6%

COOK'S NOTE: *Hummus (and pita wedges) may be warmed slightly in the microwave, if desired. For a crisper, chip-style pita, bake the chips in a 350°F oven for 6 minutes. Cool completely.*

Good source of fiber

Makes 1½ cups hummus total

Serves 6 *(¼ cup hummus and 8 chips per serving)*

SERVE WITH

3 whole-wheat pita rounds, halved crosswise (creating 6 rounds total) and cut into 8 wedges each

Calories 60; total fat 0.5g (saturated fat 0g); protein 2g; carbohydrates 12g; fiber 2g; cholesterol 0mg; sodium 120mg; vitamin A 0%; vitamin C 0%; calcium 0%; iron 4%

Two-Cheese Pimiento Topper

with Crisp Pear Slices and Cracked Pepper Crackers

Calories 150; total fat 4g (saturated fat 2.5g); protein 6g; carbohydrates 24g; fiber 3g; cholesterol 15mg; sodium 350mg; vitamin A 10%; vitamin C 15%; calcium 15%; iron 4%

¾ cup (3 ounces) finely shredded reduced-fat sharp cheddar cheese

¼ cup (approximately; 1 ounce) blue cheese, crumbled

⅔ cup fat-free sour cream

¼ cup (about 2 ounces) diced pimiento or roasted red peppers, drained

1 teaspoon Dijon mustard

½ teaspoon Worcestershire sauce

¾ teaspoon sugar

8 to 10 drops hot pepper sauce

¼ teaspoon salt

▶ Combine all the ingredients in a medium bowl. Using an electric mixer, beat on medium speed for 1 minute or until well blended. Cover with plastic wrap and refrigerate overnight.

Calories 70; total fat 3.5g (saturated fat 2.5g); protein 5g; carbohydrates 4g; fiber 0g; cholesterol 15mg; sodium 250mg; vitamin A 10%; vitamin C 8%; calcium 15%; iron 0%

> **TIME-SHAVER TIP:** *If you're brown-bagging, slice the pears in advance. Pour a little pineapple juice or squeeze a bit of any citrus juice over the pears to prevent discoloration, and store them in an airtight container.*

Good source of fiber, vitamins A and C, and calcium

Makes 1 cup cheese mixture total

Serves 8 *(2 tablespoons cheese mixture, 4 crackers, and ½ cup pear slices per serving)*

SERVE WITH

4 large firm pears, sliced (about 5 cups)

Calories 50; total fat 0g (saturated fat 0g); protein 0g; carbohydrates 13g; fiber 3g; cholesterol 0mg; sodium 0mg; vitamin A 0%; vitamin C 6%; calcium 0%; iron 0%

32 fat-free cracked pepper crackers, such as Snackwell

Calories 35; total fat 0g (saturated fat 0g); protein 1g; carbohydrates 7g; fiber 0g; cholesterol 0mg; sodium 95mg; vitamin A 0%; vitamin C 0%; calcium 2%; iron 2%

Creamy Cream Cheese with Raspberry Pepper Jelly

with Cracked Pepper Crackers

Calories 150; total fat 3.5g (saturated fat 2.5g); protein 4g; carbohydrates 26g; fiber 1g; cholesterol 10mg; sodium 170mg; vitamin A 6%; vitamin C 4%; calcium 4%; iron 2%

6 tablespoons (3 ounces) light soft cream cheese, tub style

2 tablespoons fat-free sour cream

¼ cup raspberry fruit spread

2 teaspoons balsamic vinegar

⅛ teaspoon ground cinnamon

2 tablespoons finely chopped red onion

1 medium jalapeño pepper, seeded and minced

▶ In a small bowl, combine the cream cheese and sour cream; set aside.

▶ Place the fruit spread in a small, microwave-safe bowl, and microwave on High for 20 seconds or until slightly melted. Stir in the vinegar and cinnamon, and then the onion and jalapeño. Let stand 30 minutes, if possible, to allow flavors to blend.

▶ To serve, place the bowls on a decorative plate and arrange crackers around them. Spoon the cream cheese mixture onto crackers and top with pepper jelly.

Calories 100; total fat 3.5g (saturated fat 2.5g); protein 2g; carbohydrates 14g; fiber 0g; cholesterol 10mg; sodium 105mg; vitamin A 6%; vitamin C 4%; calcium 4%; iron 0%

COOK'S NOTE: Pepper jellies are generally served over a block of cream cheese, but the method presented here is more attractive and, because of the soft texture of the cheese mixture, easier to serve.

Makes ⅓ cup pepper jelly and ½ cup cream cheese mixture total

Serves 4 *(4 teaspoons pepper jelly, 2 tablespoons cream cheese mixture, and 6 crackers per serving)*

SERVE WITH

24 fat-free cracked pepper crackers, such as Snackwell

Calories 50; total fat 0g (saturated fat 0g); protein 2g; carbohydrates 12g; fiber 1g; cholesterol 0mg; sodium 65mg; vitamin A 0%; vitamin C 0%; calcium 0%; iron 2%

Sherried Garlic Mushrooms

with Mini Phyllo Shells

Calories 140; total fat 6g (saturated fat 0g); protein 3g; carbohydrates 11g; fiber 1g; cholesterol 0mg; sodium 260mg; vitamin A 6%; vitamin C 6%; calcium 4%; iron 6%

2 tablespoons diet margarine

2 8-ounce packages sliced mushrooms, large pieces cut in half

½ teaspoon paprika

¼ teaspoon salt

⅛ teaspoon coarsely ground black pepper

4 medium green onions, chopped fine (½ cup)

1 medium garlic clove, minced

3 tablespoons dry sherry

3 tablespoons fat-free half-and-half

¼ teaspoon sugar, optional

▶ Place 1 tablespoon of the margarine in a medium nonstick skillet over medium heat, and tilt the skillet to coat the bottom evenly with the melted margarine. Add the mushrooms, paprika, salt, and pepper; cook 5 minutes or until tender, stirring frequently. Add all but 2 tablespoons of the green onion and garlic, and cook 1 minute, stirring constantly. Add the sherry, half-and-half, and sugar; cook 4 minutes or until the mixture has thickened and most of the liquid has evaporated. Sprinkle with reserved 2 tablespoons green onion. Remove from heat and stir in remaining 1 tablespoon margarine until it is melted.

Calories 70; total fat 2.5g (saturated fat 0g); protein 3g; carbohydrates 7g; fiber 1g; cholesterol 0mg; sodium 210mg; vitamin A 6%; vitamin C 6%; calcium 4%; iron 2%

COOK'S NOTE: *The mushrooms may be prepared in advance, but do not fill the shells until you are ready to serve them.*

Makes about 1 cup mushroom mixture total

Serves 4 *(4 tarts per serving)*

SERVE WITH

16 mini phyllo shells, baked according to the package directions

Calories 70; total fat 4g (saturated fat 0g); protein 0g; carbohydrates 4g; fiber 0g; cholesterol 0mg; sodium 50mg; vitamin A 0%; vitamin C 0%; calcium 0%; iron 4%

Mini Potato Bakers

Calories 150; total fat 4.5g (saturated fat 2.5g); protein 8g; carbohydrates 19g; fiber 2g; cholesterol 1mg; sodium 430mg; vitamin A 4%; vitamin C 40%; calcium 10%; iron 6%

Makes 16 potato halves total

Serves 4 (*4 potato halves per serving*)

8 medium new potatoes, scrubbed and pierced in several places with a fork

½ cup (2 ounces) finely shredded reduced-fat sharp cheddar cheese

¼ cup real bacon bits

2 medium green onions, chopped fine (¼ cup)

⅛ teaspoon salt

▶ Preheat the broiler.

▶ Place the potatoes in a shallow, microwave-safe pan, such as a deep-dish pie pan, cover with plastic wrap, and cook on High 5 minutes or until tender when pierced with a fork. Cut each in half lengthwise.

▶ Meanwhile, in a small bowl, combine the remaining ingredients and toss gently yet thoroughly to blend. Spoon equal amounts on each potato half, pressing down lightly to allow cheese mixture to adhere, and place on a cookie sheet; broil 4 inches or more from heat source, about 1 to 2 minutes or until cheese is melted and bubbly.

COOK'S NOTE: You can try to flatten the underside of each potato half before topping so they don't roll.

TIME-SHAVER TIP: Double the batch and save half for a great side dish the next night.

Excellent source of vitamin C

Good source of calcium

Pepperoni Bites

Calories 140; total fat 4g (saturated fat 2g); protein 10g; carbohydrates 15g; fiber 1g; cholesterol 20mg; sodium 470mg; vitamin A 4%; vitamin C 10%; calcium 10%; iron 6%

Makes 24 snacks total

Serves 4 *(6 snacks per serving)*

½ cup (2 ounces) finely grated Italian blend cheese or mozzarella

¼ cup finely chopped green bell pepper

¼ teaspoon dried oregano leaves

⅛ teaspoon dried pepper flakes, optional

24 garlic melba rounds

24 small turkey pepperoni slices

▶ Combine the cheese, bell pepper, oregano, and pepper flakes in a small bowl. Using a fork, toss gently yet thoroughly to blend.

▶ Arrange 12 melba rounds on a microwave-safe plate. Top with 12 pepperoni slices. Spoon a rounded teaspoon of the cheese mixture on top of each round and microwave on High 10 to 15 seconds or until cheese melts. Repeat with the remaining rounds.

TIME-SHAVER TIP: This speedy snack can be made even speedier if you combine the cheese mixture ahead of time and simply stack and microwave the rounds as needed. Double the recipe to keep plenty on hand; it's great for the kids or the workplace!

Good source of vitamin C and calcium

Jalapeño Melts

Calories 150; total fat 6g (saturated fat 2g); protein 6g; carbohydrates 18g; fiber 3g; cholesterol 5mg; sodium 310mg; vitamin A 10%; vitamin C 35%; calcium 10%; iron 6%

Makes 24 snacks total

Serves 4 *(6 snacks per serving)*

½ cup (2 ounces) finely shredded mozzarella or reduced-fat sharp cheddar cheese

12 small pitted ripe olives, chopped

2 jalapeño peppers, seeded and chopped fine

¼ cup finely chopped red bell pepper

24 reduced-fat shredded wheat crackers, such as Triscuits

▶ In a small bowl, combine the cheese, olives, and peppers; toss gently yet thoroughly to blend. Spoon equal amounts on each of the crackers. Place half of the crackers on a microwave-safe plate and microwave on High for 45 seconds or until the cheese has melted. Repeat with the remaining crackers.

COOK'S NOTE: *For additional heat, use the seeds from one of the jalapeños.*

Excellent source of vitamin C

Good source of fiber, vitamin A, and calcium

Pizza Pinchers

Calories 150; total fat 3.5g (saturated fat 2g); protein 8g; carbohydrates 20g; fiber 1g; cholesterol 10mg; sodium 470mg; vitamin A 4%; vitamin C 2%; calcium 10%; iron 6%

1 11-ounce package refrigerated French bread dough

½ cup no-salt-added tomato sauce

¼ cup chopped fresh basil leaves

⅛ teaspoon dried pepper flakes

⅛ teaspoon salt

6 ¾-ounce reduced-fat mozzarella sticks

3 tablespoons reduced-fat or regular grated Parmesan cheese

Makes 8 pizza rolls total

Serves 8 *(1 pizza roll per serving)*

▶ Preheat the oven to 400°F. Coat a nonstick baking sheet with cooking spray.

▶ On a clean work surface coated with cooking spray, roll out the French bread dough into a 12″ × 14″ rectangle. Using the back of a spoon, spread the tomato sauce evenly over the dough. Sprinkle evenly with the basil, pepper flakes, and salt.

▶ Cut the dough in half lengthwise and line up three of the cheese sticks on top of one of the dough strips to form a long roll. Repeat with the remaining cheese sticks on the other dough strip. Gently roll up the dough to make two 14-inch logs, placing the seam side down.

▶ Using a serrated knife, cut each log into four pieces. (This may be a little messy at this point.) Pinch the ends of the dough with your fingertips to seal. Using a flat spatula, place the logs about 3 inches apart on the prepared baking sheet. Bake on the center rack 10 minutes or until golden. Sprinkle evenly with the Parmesan cheese.

COOK'S NOTE: *Don't worry if some of the cheese oozes out while cooking—it makes these snacks look even more inviting!*

Good source of calcium

Antipasto Skewers

with Thin Breadsticks

Calories 150; total fat 7g (saturated fat 2g); protein 6g; carbohydrates 16g; fiber 2g; cholesterol 10mg; sodium 520mg; vitamin A 10%; vitamin C 10%; calcium 10%; iron 6%

12 wooden toothpicks

12 fresh basil leaves or small spinach leaves

½ cup (2 ounces) mozzarella, cut into 12 cubes

12 sweet grape tomatoes

12 small stuffed green olives or small pitted ripe olives

1 tablespoon light balsamic dressing

⅛ teaspoon dried rosemary leaves, crumbled

⅛ teaspoon dried pepper flakes, optional

▶ Thread each wooden pick with a folded basil leaf, a mozzarella cube, a tomato, and an olive. Place the picks on a rimmed serving plate.

▶ In a small bowl, combine the balsamic dressing, rosemary, and pepper flakes. Drizzle evenly over all, turning the picks several times to coat evenly.

Calories 80; total fat 5g (saturated fat 2g); protein 4g; carbohydrates 4g; fiber 1g; cholesterol 10mg; sodium 400mg; vitamin A 10%; vitamin C 10%; calcium 10%; iron 0%

TIME-SHAVER TIP: The skewers can be made the night before. Cover and refrigerate them until needed. Add the balsamic mixture at serving time. Flavors are at their peak if served at room temperature.

Good source of vitamins A and C and calcium

Makes 12 skewers total

Serves 4 *(3 skewers and 3 breadsticks per serving)*

SERVE WITH

12 thin breadsticks, about ⅜" × 9", such as Alessi

Calories 70; total fat 1.5g (saturated fat 0g); protein 2g; carbohydrates 12g; fiber 1g; cholesterol 0mg; sodium 120mg; vitamin A 0%; vitamin C 0%; calcium 0%; iron 4%

Salmon-Topped Cucumber Rounds

with Thin Breadsticks

Calories 150; total fat 4g (saturated fat 1g); protein 10g; carbohydrates 18g; fiber 1g; cholesterol 55mg; sodium 310mg; vitamin A 8%; vitamin C 6%; calcium 8%; iron 8%

½ cup fat-free sour cream

3 tablespoons capers, drained

3 tablespoons finely chopped red onion

¾ teaspoon chopped fresh dill weed or ¼ teaspoon dried
  dill weed

1½ medium cucumbers, peeled and cut into 24 slices

1 3-ounce pouch smoked salmon, such as Alaskan Pacific

1 large hard-boiled egg, peeled and chopped fine

▶ Combine the sour cream, capers, onion, and dill in a small
  bowl; stir gently yet thoroughly until well blended. Spoon
  equal amounts on the cucumber rounds, and sprinkle each
  with even amounts of the salmon and egg.

Calories 100; total fat 3g (saturated fat 0.5g); protein 9g; carbohydrates 9g; fiber 1g; cholesterol 55mg; sodium 230mg; vitamin A 8%; vitamin C 6%; calcium 8%; iron 6%

Makes about ¾ cup sour cream mixture total

Serves 4 *(6 rounds and 2 breadsticks per serving)*

SERVE WITH

8 thin breadsticks, about ⅜″ × 9″, such as Alessi

Calories 50; total fat 1g (saturated fat 0g); protein 1g; carbohydrates 8g; fiber 0g; cholesterol 0mg; sodium 80mg; vitamin A 0%; vitamin C 0%; calcium 0%; iron 2%

TIME-SHAVER TIP: *Entertaining but have no time to assemble the rounds? Place all the ingredients in small bowls and let everyone build their own!*

Cheese Bundles

Calories 140; total fat 5g (saturated fat 3g); protein 13g; carbohydrates 8g; fiber 2g; cholesterol 20mg; sodium 410mg; vitamin A 50%; vitamin C 160%; calcium 30%; iron 4%

Makes 16 bundles total

Serves 4 *(4 bundles per serving)*

3 tablespoons honey mustard

¼ teaspoon Louisiana hot sauce

¼ teaspoon curry powder

16 medium leaves Boston or Bibb lettuce

8 ¾-ounce reduced-fat mozzarella cheese sticks, cut in half lengthwise

1 large red bell pepper, cut into thin strips (about 1½ cups)

2 cups alfalfa sprouts

16 toothpicks

▶ In a small bowl, combine the mustard, hot sauce, and curry powder. Spoon equal amounts (about ½ teaspoon) of the mustard mixture down the center of each lettuce leaf. Place a halved cheese stick on the center of each, and top with pepper strips and sprouts. Roll the lettuce leaves and secure with the toothpicks.

COOK'S NOTE: *This is a great one for entertaining but can also be used as a side with a hot bowl of soup for lunch or dinner.*

Excellent source of vitamins A and C and calcium

Double-Stuffed Deviled Eggs

Calories 140; total fat 5g (saturated fat 1g); protein 12g; carbohydrates 11g; fiber 2g; cholesterol 110mg; sodium 370mg; vitamin A 4%; vitamin C 0%; calcium 4%; iron 6%

Makes 16 deviled egg halves total

Serves 4 *(4 egg halves per serving)*

8 large hard-boiled eggs, peeled and halved

½ 15.5-ounce can navy beans, rinsed and drained

2 tablespoons light mayonnaise

2 tablespoons fat-free sour cream

1 to 2 tablespoons sweet pickle relish

½ to 1 teaspoon prepared mustard

8 drops hot pepper sauce or to taste

Paprika

▶ Place four of the egg yolk halves in a blender or small food processor, discarding the remaining yolks. Add the beans, mayonnaise, sour cream, relish, mustard, and hot sauce; puree until smooth.

▶ Spoon equal amounts of the egg mixture into each of the egg white halves; sprinkle evenly with paprika.

COOK'S NOTE: *Having trouble with your eggs breaking while cooking? Put the eggs in a saucepan, cover with cold water, and bring it to a boil. Reduce the heat and simmer 10 minutes. Eggs break when you add them to hot water.*

3

Lunches

SOUPS

- ▶ Chipotle Chicken and Hominy Chili Soup
- ▶ Black Bean–Poblano Chili Soup
- ▶ Smoked White Bean Soup
- ▶ Fresh Basil, Tomato, and Navy Bean Soup
- ▶ Chunky Ham and String Bean Soup
- ▶ Creamy Shrimp and Corn Soup Bowls
- ▶ Weeklong Lunch Soup
- ▶ Curried Pumpkin Bisque

SALADS

- ▶ Shrimp Salad in Creamy Cocktail Dressing
- ▶ Curried Chicken–Water Chestnut Salad
- ▶ Tuna-Egg Salads on Greens
- ▶ Chicken–Green Bean Pasta Salad and Blue Cheese
- ▶ Protein Potato Salad
- ▶ Mozzarella and Bean Salad
- ▶ Chef's Chopped Salad
- ▶ Chicken–Goat Cheese Spinach Salad and Raspberry Dressing

HOT SANDWICHES

- ▶ Flash-Fix Crunchy Tortilla Rounds
- ▶ Salsa Verde Pork Tortilla Flats
- ▶ So Sloppy Turkey Joes
- ▶ Smoked Sausage Fryers
- ▶ Ground Beef and Sausage Burgers
- ▶ Easy Provolone, Basil, and Kalamata Paninis
- ▶ Spring Greens and Swiss Chicken on English Muffins
- ▶ Grilled Ham, Onion, and Rye

COLD SANDWICHES

- ▶ Country Herbed-Cheese Crostini
- ▶ Lemon Vinaigrette Greens on Italian Bread
- ▶ Avocado, Feta, and Sprout Pitas
- ▶ Chicken-Almond Hoisin Wraps
- ▶ Unwrapped Roast Beef and Blue Cheese Wraps
- ▶ Hummus, Swiss, and Rye Crispbreads

Chipotle Chicken and Hominy Chili Soup

with Creamy Country Coleslaw and Fresh Pineapple

Calories 340; total fat 8g (saturated fat 1.5g); protein 24g; carbohydrates 45g; fiber 7g; cholesterol 55mg; sodium 1,070mg; vitamin A 60%; vitamin C 170%; calcium 10%; iron 20%

1 tablespoon extra-virgin olive oil

¾ pound boneless, skinless chicken breast, cut into ½-inch pieces

1 14-ounce can reduced-sodium chicken broth

½ 15.5-ounce can hominy (or corn), rinsed and drained

1 medium carrot, sliced thin (about ⅔ cup)

1 14.5-ounce can stewed tomatoes with Mexican seasonings

½ to 1 chipotle pepper, minced

2 tablespoons chopped fresh cilantro

▶ Heat a large saucepan over medium heat until hot. Coat the pan with cooking spray; add 1 teaspoon of the oil and tilt the pan to coat lightly. Add the chicken and cook 2 minutes or until it is no longer pink on the outside, stirring constantly. Remove the chicken from the pan and set aside on a separate plate.

▶ Combine the broth, hominy, carrot, tomatoes, and chipotle in the saucepan. Bring to a boil over high heat; reduce the heat, cover, and simmer 20 minutes. Add the chicken and remaining 2 teaspoons oil; cook 2 minutes to heat thoroughly and blend the flavors. Top with the cilantro.

Calories 190; total fat 4.5g (saturated fat 1g); protein 23g; carbohydrates 15g; fiber 3g; cholesterol 50mg; sodium 780mg; vitamin A 60%; vitamin C 20%; calcium 4%; iron 15%

TIME-SHAVER TIP: *Instead of cooking the chicken yourself, you can substitute 2 cups chopped cooked chicken breast from a supermarket rotisserie chicken or a frozen precooked bag.*

Excellent source of fiber and vitamins A and C

Good source of calcium and iron

Makes 5 cups soup total

Serves 4 *(1¼ cups soup, 1 cup coleslaw, 1 tablespoon dressing, and 1 cup diced pineapple per serving)*

SERVE WITH

4 cups coleslaw mix tossed with ¼ cup reduced-fat coleslaw dressing

Calories 70; total fat 3.5g (saturated fat 0.5g); protein 1g; carbohydrates 11g; fiber 2g; cholesterol 5mg; sodium 280mg; vitamin A 2%; vitamin C 60%; calcium 4%; iron 2%

4 cups diced fresh pineapple

Calories 70; total fat 0g (saturated fat 0g); protein 1g; carbohydrates 20g; fiber 2g; cholesterol 0mg; sodium 0mg; vitamin A 2%; vitamin C 90%; calcium 2%; iron 2%

74

Black Bean–Poblano Chili Soup

with Lettuce Shreds with Sour Cream and Picante, Cheese Crackers, and Orange Sections

Calories 350; total fat 5g (saturated fat 1.5g); protein 31g; carbohydrates 47g; fiber 9g; cholesterol 35mg; sodium 770mg; vitamin A 90%; vitamin C 180%; calcium 15%; iron 25%

¾ pound 99% fat-free ground turkey breast

2 poblano chili peppers or 1 large green pepper, seeded and chopped (about 1½ cups)

1 15-ounce can black beans, rinsed and drained

1 14.5-ounce can stewed tomatoes with Mexican seasonings

1 cup water

1 tablespoon instant coffee granules

2 teaspoons chili powder

▶ Heat a Dutch oven over medium-high heat until hot and coat with cooking spray. Add the turkey and peppers, coat them with cooking spray, and cook until the turkey is no longer pink, stirring constantly. Add the remaining ingredients and bring to a boil. Reduce the heat, cover, and simmer 20 minutes or until peppers are very tender, stirring occasionally and breaking up the larger pieces of tomato.

Calories 190; total fat 2g (saturated fat 0g); protein 26g; carbohydrates 20g; fiber 5g; cholesterol 35mg; sodium 510mg; vitamin A 15%; vitamin C 80%; calcium 6%; iron 20%

COOK'S NOTE: There's a considerable difference in the number of fat grams found in the various kinds of ground turkey on supermarket shelves. The leanest is the ground turkey breast.

Excellent source of fiber, vitamins A and C, and iron

Good source of calcium

Makes 5 cups soup total

Serves 4 *(1¼ cups soup, 1 cup lettuce, 2 tablespoons sour cream, 1 tablespoon picante sauce, ¼ cup crackers, and ½ cup orange sections per serving)*

SERVE WITH

4 cups shredded lettuce topped with ½ cup fat-free sour cream and ¼ cup picante sauce

Calories 45; total fat 0.5g (saturated fat 0g); protein 2g; carbohydrates 8g; fiber 2g; cholesterol 5mg; sodium 140mg; vitamin A 70%; vitamin C 25%; calcium 6%; iron 4%

1 cup (2 ounces) goldfish-style crackers, such as Pepperidge Farm Goldfish

Calories 70; total fat 3g (saturated fat 1g); protein 1g; carbohydrates 9g; fiber 0g; cholesterol 0mg; sodium 110mg; vitamin A 0%; vitamin C 0%; calcium 0%; iron 2%

2 cups orange sections

Calories 40; total fat 0g (saturated fat 0g); protein 1g; carbohydrates 11g; fiber 2g; cholesterol 0mg; sodium 0mg; vitamin A 4%; vitamin C 80%; calcium 4%; iron 0%

Smoked White Bean Soup

with Mixed Green Salad with Olive Oil Vinaigrette, Breadsticks, and Fresh Nectarines

Calories 350; total fat 12g (saturated fat 1.5g); protein 15g; carbohydrates 48g; fiber 9g; cholesterol 10mg; sodium 1,160mg; vitamin A 90%; vitamin C 170%; calcium 8%; iron 20%

1 cup (¼ pound) 96% fat-free cooked diced ham

1½ medium yellow onions, chopped (1½ cups)

1 cup matchstick carrots

1 14-ounce can reduced-sodium chicken broth

1 cup water

½ 15.5-ounce can navy beans, rinsed and drained

½ teaspoon dried thyme leaves

1½ teaspoons liquid smoke

▶ Heat a large saucepan over medium-high heat until hot, and coat with cooking spray. Add the ham and cook 2 minutes or until lightly browned, stirring frequently. Set aside on a separate plate.

▶ Recoat the saucepan with cooking spray, and add the onions and carrots. Coat the vegetables with cooking spray, reduce heat to medium, and cook 5 minutes or until onions are translucent, stirring frequently. Add the remaining ingredients, except the liquid smoke, and bring to a boil over high heat; reduce heat, cover, and simmer 15 minutes. Remove from heat, add the liquid smoke, and let stand 5 minutes to absorb the flavors.

Calories 110; total fat 1.5g (saturated fat 0g); protein 10g; carbohydrates 15g; fiber 3g; cholesterol 10mg; sodium 760mg; vitamin A 35%; vitamin C 8%; calcium 4%; iron 8%

TIME-SHAVER TIP: Look for diced ham in the meat section of your supermarket; it is generally sold near the smoked hams. You can freeze the leftovers to use another time.

Excellent source of fiber, vitamins A and C, and iron

Makes about 5 cups soup total

Serves 4 *(about 1¼ cups soup, 1½ cups salad, 1 tablespoon vinaigrette, 4 breadsticks, and ½ cup nectarine slices per serving)*

SERVE WITH

4 cups mixed greens topped with 1 medium red bell pepper, chopped (1 cup); 1 avocado, seeded and chopped (1 cup); and ¼ cup light olive oil vinaigrette

Calories 100; total fat 8g (saturated fat 1g); protein 2g; carbohydrates 8g; fiber 5g; cholesterol 0mg; sodium 250mg; vitamin A 60%; vitamin C 160%; calcium 4%; iron 6%

16 thin breadsticks, such as Alessi

Calories 100; total fat 2.5g (saturated fat 0g); protein 3g; carbohydrates 16g; fiber 1g; cholesterol 0mg; sodium 160mg; vitamin A 0%; vitamin C 0%; calcium 0%; iron 6%

2 medium nectarines or peaches, pitted and sliced (2 cups)

Calories 35; total fat 0g (saturated fat 0g); protein 1g; carbohydrates 8g; fiber 1g; cholesterol 0mg; sodium 0mg; vitamin A 2%; vitamin C 8%; calcium 0%; iron 2%

Fresh Basil, Tomato, and Navy Bean Soup

with Crusty French Bread with Olive Oil, Balsamic Spring Greens, and Sweet Grapes

Calories 340; total fat 10g (saturated fat 1.5g); protein 10g; carbohydrates 58g; fiber 9g; cholesterol 0mg; sodium 1,230mg; vitamin A 80%; vitamin C 45%; calcium 15%; iron 20%

1 14.5-ounce can stewed tomatoes with Italian seasonings

½ cup matchstick carrots

1 15.5-ounce can navy beans, rinsed and drained

2 cups water

1 cup (2 ounces) packed fresh baby spinach

¼ cup chopped fresh basil

1 tablespoon extra-virgin olive oil

⅛ teaspoon dried pepper flakes, optional

¼ teaspoon salt

Freshly ground black pepper to taste

▶ Combine the tomatoes, carrots, beans, and water in a large saucepan; bring to a boil over high heat. Reduce heat, cover, and simmer 20 minutes, stirring occasionally and breaking up the larger pieces of tomato.

▶ Remove from heat and stir in the remaining ingredients. Cover and let stand 5 to 10 minutes to absorb flavors.

Calories 150; total fat 4g (saturated fat 0.5g); protein 7g; carbohydrates 23g; fiber 6g; cholesterol 0mg; sodium 830mg; vitamin A 50%; vitamin C 15%; calcium 6%; iron 10%

TIME-SHAVER TIP: The only thing that is chopped in this recipe is the small amount of basil. Taking advantage of precut fruits, veggies, meats, and a wide variety of canned items will help cut your meal preparation time!

Excellent source of fiber, vitamins A and C, and iron

Good source of calcium

Makes about 4 cups soup total

Serves 4 *(1 cup soup, 1 bread slice, 1 teaspoon olive oil, 1 cup salad, 1 tablespoon dressing, and ½ cup grapes per serving)*

SERVE WITH

4 ounces French bread, sliced, heated, and drizzled with 4 teaspoons extra-virgin olive oil

Calories 120; total fat 6g (saturated fat 1g); protein 2g; carbohydrates 15g; fiber 1g; cholesterol 0mg; sodium 150mg; vitamin A 0%; vitamin C 0%; calcium 4%; iron 4%

4 cups spring greens tossed with ¼ cup fat-free balsamic salad dressing

Calories 25; total fat 0g (saturated fat 0g); protein 1g; carbohydrates 6g; fiber 1g; cholesterol 0mg; sodium 240mg; vitamin A 30%; vitamin C 15%; calcium 4%; iron 4%

2 cups seedless grapes

Calories 60; total fat 0g (saturated fat 0g); protein 1g; carbohydrates 14g; fiber 1g; cholesterol 0mg; sodium 0mg; vitamin A 2%; vitamin C 15%; calcium 0%; iron 2%

Chunky Ham and String Bean Soup

with Buttery Rye Bread, Crisp Apple Slices, and Cold Milk

Calories 350; total fat 8g (saturated fat 3.5g); protein 29g; carbohydrates 43g; fiber 6g; cholesterol 35mg; sodium 1,120mg; vitamin A 50%; vitamin C 130%; calcium 45%; iron 10%

2 cups (approximately; ½ pound) 96% fat-free diced ham

1 cup (5 ounces) frozen cut green beans

4 medium green onions, chopped fine (½ cup)

1 medium red bell pepper, chopped (1 cup)

½ cup water

1¾ cups fat-free milk

½ cup dry instant mashed potatoes

¼ teaspoon coarsely ground black pepper

½ cup (2 ounces) shredded reduced-fat sharp cheddar cheese

▶ Heat a large saucepan over medium heat until hot, and coat the pan with cooking spray. Add the ham and cook 4 minutes or until beginning to brown lightly and any liquid has evaporated. Add the beans, all but 2 tablespoons of the onion, the bell pepper, and the water. Bring to a boil over high heat; reduce heat, cover, and simmer 10 minutes or until beans are very tender.

▶ Stir in the milk, potatoes, and black pepper. Cook, uncovered, 5 minutes on medium-low heat to warm through. Serve topped with cheese and the remaining 2 tablespoons onion.

Calories 190; total fat 6g (saturated fat 3g); protein 20g; carbohydrates 16g; fiber 2g; cholesterol 35mg; sodium 900mg; vitamin A 35%; vitamin C 130%; calcium 25%; iron 8%

COOK'S NOTE: *Using instant potatoes as a thickening agent instead of flour helps to achieve the desired texture and body of this dish.*

Excellent source of fiber, vitamins A and C, and calcium

Good source of iron

Makes 4 cups soup total

Serves 4 *(1 cup soup, 1 bread slice, 1 teaspoon margarine, ½ cup sliced apples, and ¾ cup milk per serving)*

SERVE WITH

4 slices reduced-calorie rye bread topped with 4 teaspoons diet margarine

Calories 60; total fat 2g (saturated fat 0g); protein 2g; carbohydrates 10g; fiber 3g; cholesterol 0mg; sodium 125mg; vitamin A 4%; vitamin C 0%; calcium 2%; iron 4%

2 medium apples, sliced (2 cups)

Calories 30; total fat 0g (saturated fat 0g); protein 0g; carbohydrates 8g; fiber 1g; cholesterol 0mg; sodium 0mg; vitamin A 0%; vitamin C 4%; calcium 0%; iron 0%

3 cups fat-free milk

Calories 70; total fat 0g (saturated fat 0g); protein 7g; carbohydrates 10g; fiber 0g; cholesterol 0mg; sodium 100mg; vitamin A 8%; vitamin C 2%; calcium 20%; iron 0%

Creamy Shrimp and Corn Soup Bowls

with Tomato-Cucumber Salad, Fresh Oranges, and Wheat Crackers

Calories 350; total fat 5g (saturated fat 2g); protein 24g; carbohydrates 55g; fiber 8g; cholesterol 95mg; sodium 1,000mg; vitamin A 60%; vitamin C 270%; calcium 30%; iron 15%

1½ medium yellow onions, chopped fine (1½ cups)

1 medium red bell pepper, chopped (1 cup)

1 cup (5 ounces) frozen corn

2 cups fat-free milk

½ teaspoon seafood seasoning, such as Old Bay

½ pound raw medium shrimp, peeled

¼ cup (2 ounces) light cream cheese, tub style, cut into small pieces

½ teaspoon salt

▶ Heat a large saucepan over medium heat until hot, and coat the saucepan with cooking spray. Add the onion, coat with cooking spray, and cook 4 minutes or until it is translucent, stirring frequently. Add the bell pepper, corn, milk, and seafood seasoning. Increase the heat to medium high and bring to a simmer; reduce heat, cover, and simmer 10 minutes.

▶ Increase the heat to medium, add the shrimp and cook, uncovered, 5 minutes, stirring frequently. Remove from heat, stir in the cream cheese and salt, and let stand 5 minutes or until the cheese has melted.

Calories 210; total fat 3.5g (saturated fat 2g); protein 19g; carbohydrates 25g; fiber 3g; cholesterol 95mg; sodium 670mg; vitamin A 35%; vitamin C 130%; calcium 20%; iron 10%

TIME-SHAVER TIP: Adding the cream cheese at the end gives a rich, creamy texture to the soup without having to use flour or butter—and it's a lot easier and faster too!

Excellent source of fiber, vitamins A and C, and calcium

Good source of iron

Makes 4 cups soup total

Serves 4 *(1 cup soup, 1 cup salad, 1 tablespoon dressing, 1 orange, and 4 crackers per serving)*

SERVE WITH

2 cups cherry tomatoes, halved (10 ounces), and 1 medium cucumber, peeled and diced (2 cups), tossed with ¼ cup fat-free Italian dressing

Calories 35; total fat 0g (saturated fat 0g); protein 2g; carbohydrates 7g; fiber 2g; cholesterol 0mg; sodium 220mg; vitamin A 20%; vitamin C 25%; calcium 2%; iron 2%

4 medium oranges

Calories 60; total fat 0g (saturated fat 0g); protein 1g; carbohydrates 15g; fiber 3g; cholesterol 0mg; sodium 0mg; vitamin A 6%; vitamin C 120%; calcium 6%; iron 0%

16 stoned wheat crackers

Calories 50; total fat 1g (saturated fat 0g); protein 2g; carbohydrates 8g; fiber 1g; cholesterol 0mg; sodium 110mg; vitamin A 0%; vitamin C 0%; calcium 2%; iron 2%

Weeklong Lunch Soup

with Corn Muffins and Watermelon

Calories 350; total fat 8g (saturated fat 2.5g); protein 14g; carbohydrates 57g; fiber 5g; cholesterol 30mg; sodium 960mg; vitamin A 90%; vitamin C 70%; calcium 4%; iron 15%

½ pound reduced-fat Italian turkey sausage

1 14.5-ounce can reduced-sodium beef broth

2 cups (½ pound) potatoes, scrubbed and diced

½ 16-ounce package frozen pepper stir-fry

2 cups frozen mixed vegetables

1 14.5-ounce can diced tomatoes

1 cup water

1 teaspoon Worcestershire sauce

3 tablespoons ketchup

▶ Heat a Dutch oven over medium-high heat until hot. Add the sausage and cook until browned, stirring constantly. Add all remaining ingredients, except the ketchup. Increase heat to high and bring to a boil; reduce heat, cover, and simmer 15 minutes.

▶ Remove from heat, stir in the ketchup, and let stand uncovered 5 minutes to absorb flavors and thicken slightly.

Calories 160; total fat 4.5g (saturated fat 1.5g); protein 10g; carbohydrates 20g; fiber 3g; cholesterol 25mg; sodium 680mg; vitamin A 70%; vitamin C 45%; calcium 2%; iron 10%

TIME-SHAVER TIP: *This is a great soup. You can pack it in a thermos or in freezer bags in individual portions for when you need it.*

Excellent source of vitamins A and C and fiber

Good source of iron

Makes 8 cups soup total

Serves 6 *(1⅓ cups soup, 1 muffin, and 1 cup watermelon cubes per serving)*

SERVE WITH

6 corn muffins

> Calories 150; total fat 3.5g (saturated fat 1g); protein 3g; carbohydrates 26g; fiber 1g; cholesterol 5mg; sodium 280mg; vitamin A 0%; vitamin C 0%; calcium 0%; iron 2%

6 cups watermelon cubes

> Calories 45; total fat 0g (saturated fat 0g); protein 1g; carbohydrates 11g; fiber 1g; cholesterol 0mg; sodium 0mg; vitamin A 15%; vitamin C 20%; calcium 2%; iron 2%

Curried Pumpkin Bisque

with Turkey-Spinach and Swiss Country Sandwich Halves and Apple Slices

Calories 340; total fat 7g (saturated fat 3g); protein 20g; carbohydrates 54g; fiber 8g; cholesterol 25mg; sodium 1,190mg; vitamin A 520%; vitamin C 25%; calcium 35%; iron 20%

1 medium yellow onion, chopped fine (1 cup)

1 14.5-ounce can reduced-sodium chicken broth

1 15-ounce can solid pumpkin

2½ teaspoons sugar

1 teaspoon curry powder

1 cup fat-free half-and-half

1 tablespoon diet margarine

½ teaspoon salt, optional

¼ teaspoon cayenne, optional

¼ cup chopped fresh cilantro

▶ Heat a large saucepan over medium heat until hot, and coat the saucepan with cooking spray. Add the onion, coat with cooking spray, and cook 4 minutes or until it is translucent, stirring frequently. Add the broth, pumpkin, sugar, and curry powder; whisk together until well blended. Increase heat to medium high and bring to a boil; reduce heat, cover, and simmer 20 minutes or until onion is tender, stirring occasionally.

▶ Remove from heat; stir in all remaining ingredients, except the cilantro. Sprinkle the cilantro over all.

Calories 120; total fat 1.5g (saturated fat 0g); protein 5g; carbohydrates 22g; fiber 4g; cholesterol 0mg; sodium 580mg; vitamin A 510%; vitamin C 15%; calcium 15%; iron 10%

> 🥄 **COOK'S NOTE:** *For a variation, bake and mash 1 pound fresh sweet potato to use in place of the pumpkin. This is a great way to use up leftover sweet potatoes.*

Excellent source of fiber, vitamins A and C, calcium, and iron

---

Makes 5 cups soup total

Serves 4 *(1¼ cups soup, 1 sandwich, and ¾ cup apple slices per serving)*

SERVE WITH

4 1-ounce slices country French bread, halved; 8 teaspoons stone-ground mustard; 4 slices reduced-fat Swiss cheese; ¼ pound (4 ounces) oven-roasted turkey; ½ medium red onion, sliced thin (½ cup); and 2 cups baby spinach: makes 4 sandwiches

Calories 180; total fat 6g (saturated fat 2.5g); protein 15g; carbohydrates 20g; fiber 2g; cholesterol 25mg; sodium 600mg; vitamin A 15%; vitamin C 4%; calcium 25%; iron 8%

3 medium apples, sliced (3 cups)

Calories 45; total fat 0g (saturated fat 0g); protein 0g; carbohydrates 11g; fiber 2g; cholesterol 0mg; sodium 0mg; vitamin A 0%; vitamin C 6%; calcium 0%; iron 0%

Shrimp Salad in Creamy Cocktail Dressing

with Tortilla Chips with Avocado and Tomatoes

Calories 350; total fat 11g (saturated fat 1.5g); protein 27g; carbohydrates 38g; fiber 7g; cholesterol 175mg; sodium 850mg; vitamin A 25%; vitamin C 45%; calcium 15%; iron 20%

4 cups water

1 tablespoon liquid shrimp and crab boil, such as Zatarain's

1 pound raw medium shrimp, peeled

2 medium celery stalks, sliced thin (1 cup)

2 tablespoons light mayonnaise

1 tablespoon fat-free sour cream

2 tablespoons ketchup

2 teaspoons horseradish

1 tablespoon lemon juice

1 teaspoon Worcestershire sauce, optional

½ teaspoon salt

1 medium lemon, quartered

Makes 3 cups salad total

Serves 4 (¾ cup shrimp salad, 1 ounce chips, plus 1 cup avocado and tomato mixture per serving)

SERVE WITH

4 ounces low-fat tortilla chips

Calories 110; total fat 1g (saturated fat 0g); protein 2g; carbohydrates 24g; fiber 2g; cholesterol 0mg; sodium 200mg; vitamin A 0%; vitamin C 0%; calcium 4%; iron 2%

1 ripe medium avocado, diced (1 cup) and tossed with 1 pound tomatoes, diced (4 cups)

Calories 80; total fat 6g (saturated fat 1g); protein 2g; carbohydrates 8g; fiber 4g; cholesterol 0mg; sodium 10mg; vitamin A 20%; vitamin C 30%; calcium 2%; iron 2%

▶ Bring the water to a boil in a large saucepan over high heat. Add the shrimp and crab boil and shrimp, return to a boil, and cook 3 minutes or until shrimp are opaque in the center. Drain and place on a sheet of foil in a single layer to cool quickly, about 5 to 8 minutes.

▶ Meanwhile, combine all remaining ingredients except lemon in a medium bowl. Add the shrimp and stir until well blended. Serve with lemon wedges.

Calories 160; total fat 4.5g (saturated fat 0g); protein 24g; carbohydrates 6g; fiber 1g; cholesterol 175mg; sodium 640mg; vitamin A 6%; vitamin C 15%; calcium 8%; iron 15%

COOK'S NOTE: *For a variation, roll smaller amounts of the salad in Boston or Bibb lettuce leaves and serve as wraps.*

Excellent source of fiber, vitamins A and C, and iron

Good source of calcium

Curried Chicken–Water Chestnut Salad

with Red Pepper Strips and Fresh Pear Slices

Calories 350; total fat 12g (saturated fat 1g); protein 29g; carbohydrates 32g; fiber 6g; cholesterol 75mg; sodium 340mg; vitamin A 20%; vitamin C 120%; calcium 6%; iron 10%

2½ cups (¾ pound) cooked diced chicken breast

¼ cup diet mayonnaise

¾ teaspoon curry powder

¼ teaspoon ground cumin

⅛ teaspoon salt

1 8-ounce can sliced water chestnuts, drained and chopped

½ cup golden raisins

¼ cup (approximately; 1 ounce) sliced almonds, toasted

▶ Combine the chicken, mayonnaise, curry powder, cumin, and salt in a large bowl; stir until well blended. Add the remaining ingredients and stir until just blended. Let stand 15 minutes to absorb flavors and to allow the curry to give the salad a yellowish color.

Calories 310; total fat 12g (saturated fat 1g); protein 29g; carbohydrates 22g; fiber 3g; cholesterol 75mg; sodium 340mg; vitamin A 0%; vitamin C 2%; calcium 4%; iron 8%

Excellent source of fiber and vitamins A and C

Good source of iron

Makes 4 cups salad total

Serves 4 *(1 cup salad, ⅓ cup red pepper, and ¼ cup pear per serving)*

SERVE WITH

1 large red bell pepper, cut into strips (1½ cups)

Calories 10; total fat 0g (saturated fat 0g); protein 0g; carbohydrates 2g; fiber 1g; cholesterol 0mg; sodium 0mg; vitamin A 20%; vitamin C 110%; calcium 0%; iron 0%

1 medium pear, sliced (1 cup)

Calories 30; total fat 0g (saturated fat 0g); protein 0g; carbohydrates 8g; fiber 2g; cholesterol 0mg; sodium 0mg; vitamin A 0%; vitamin C 4%; calcium 0%; iron 0%

Tuna-Egg Salads on Greens

with Diced Cantaloupe and Fresh Raspberries

Calories 340; total fat 11g (saturated fat 1g); protein 31g; carbohydrates 30g; fiber 4g; cholesterol 170mg; sodium 900mg; vitamin A 130%; vitamin C 120%; calcium 8%; iron 8%

2 6-ounce cans tuna in water, rinsed and drained

¼ cup plus 2 tablespoons diet mayonnaise

¼ cup fat-free sour cream

¼ cup sweet pickle relish

1 teaspoon prepared mustard

¼ teaspoon salt

4 large hard-boiled eggs, 2 yolks discarded, chopped

2 medium celery stalks, chopped fine (about 1 cup total)

4 cups spring greens

▶ Combine the tuna, mayonnaise, sour cream, relish, mustard, and salt; stir until well blended. Stir in the eggs and celery until blended. Let stand 10 minutes to absorb flavors, and serve over individual beds of greens.

Calories 270; total fat 10g (saturated fat 1g); protein 29g; carbohydrates 13g; fiber 1g; cholesterol 170mg; sodium 870mg; vitamin A 20%; vitamin C 8%; calcium 6%; iron 6%

COOK'S NOTE: *Be sure to rinse the tuna under water and drain it, pressing out any excess liquid for peak flavors and texture.*

Excellent source of vitamins A and C

Good source of fiber

Makes 2 cups tuna-egg salad total

Serves 4 *(½ cup tuna-egg salad, 1 cup spring greens, 1 cup cantaloupe, and ¼ cup raspberries per serving)*

SERVE WITH

4 cups diced cantaloupe topped with 1 cup fresh raspberries

Calories 70; total fat 0g (saturated fat 0g); protein 2g; carbohydrates 16g; fiber 3g; cholesterol 0mg; sodium 25mg; vitamin A 110%; vitamin C 110%; calcium 2%; iron 2%

Chicken–Green Bean Pasta Salad and Blue Cheese

with Baby Spinach and Fruit Juice Blend Fizzer

Calories 350; total fat 9g (saturated fat 2.5g); protein 30g; carbohydrates 41g; fiber 7g; cholesterol 65mg; sodium 490mg; vitamin A 25%; vitamin C 120%; calcium 10%; iron 15%

4 ounces whole-wheat or multigrain rotini

6 ounces whole green beans, stems removed, halved (about 1½ cups)

2 cups (about 10 ounces) diced cooked chicken breast

½ medium red onion, sliced thin (½ cup)

¼ cup light olive oil vinaigrette

½ teaspoon Dijon mustard

1 tablespoon fresh or 1 teaspoon dried oregano

¼ teaspoon salt

¼ teaspoon black pepper

¼ cup (1 ounce) reduced-fat crumbled blue cheese

▶ Cook the pasta according to the package directions, omitting any salt or fat. Add the beans during the last 4 minutes of cooking. Drain well and run under cold water to cool quickly. Shake off any excess liquid.

▶ Meanwhile, combine the remaining ingredients, except the blue cheese, in a large bowl. Toss to coat evenly. Add the cooled pasta mixture and toss gently yet thoroughly to blend well. Add the cheese and toss gently. Let stand 5 minutes to absorb flavors.

Calories 300; total fat 9g (saturated fat 2.5g); protein 29g; carbohydrates 29g; fiber 6g; cholesterol 65mg; sodium 430mg; vitamin A 10%; vitamin C 15%; calcium 10%; iron 10%

TIME-SHAVER TIP: *Adding the beans during the last few minutes of pasta cooking saves not only time but an extra pot as well.*

Excellent source of fiber and vitamins A and C

Good source of calcium and iron

Makes 6 cups pasta salad total

Serves 4 *(1½ cups pasta salad, 1 cup spinach, and 1½ cups juice mixture per serving)*

SERVE WITH

4 cups baby spinach (as a bed for the salad)

Calories 10; total fat 0g (saturated fat 0g); protein 1g; carbohydrates 3g; fiber 1g; cholesterol 0mg; sodium 40mg; vitamin A 15%; vitamin C 6%; calcium 2%; iron 4%

4 cups light orange, strawberry, and banana juice mixed with 2 cups diet ginger ale

Calories 35; total fat 0g (saturated fat 0g); protein 1g; carbohydrates 9g; fiber 0g; cholesterol 0mg; sodium 20mg; vitamin A 0%; vitamin C 100%; calcium 0%; iron 0%

Protein Potato Salad

with Asparagus Spears and Nectarine Slices

Calories 350; total fat 12g (saturated fat 0.5g); protein 16g; carbohydrates 47g; fiber 7g; cholesterol 35mg; sodium 940mg; vitamin A 20%; vitamin C 80%; calcium 6%; iron 25%

2 cups (½ pound) diced extra-lean ham

8 cups water

1½ pounds red potatoes, scrubbed and cut into ½-inch cubes (6 cups)

½ cup light mayonnaise

2 teaspoons prepared mustard or to taste

1½ medium celery stalks, chopped fine (1½ cups)

½ medium yellow onion, chopped fine (½ cup)

Freshly ground black pepper to taste

▶ Place a Dutch oven over medium-high heat until hot, and coat it with cooking spray. Add the ham, and cook 3 to 4 minutes or until beginning to brown, stirring occasionally. Remove from the Dutch oven and place in a large bowl; set aside.

▶ Add the water to any pan residue in the Dutch oven and bring to a boil over high heat. Add the potatoes, return to a boil, and continue to boil 5 minutes or until potatoes are tender.

▶ Meanwhile, combine the mayonnaise, mustard, celery, and onion in the large bowl with the ham. Stir until well blended and set aside.

▶ Drain the potatoes in a colander and run under cold water until cool; shake off any excess liquid and add to the ham mixture. Stir gently yet thoroughly until well blended. Top with black pepper.

Calories 300; total fat 12g (saturated fat 0.5g); protein 13g; carbohydrates 35g; fiber 4g; cholesterol 35mg; sodium 930mg; vitamin A 2%; vitamin C 60%; calcium 4%; iron 10%

TIME-SHAVER TIP: *Cook the potatoes in the same pot the ham was cooked in. This not only saves you cleaning an extra pot but also adds a bit more flavor to the potatoes and cleans the cooked-on particles.*

Excellent source of fiber, vitamins A and C, and iron

Makes 6 cups salad total

Serves 4 *(1½ cups salad, 4 ounces asparagus, and ½ cup nectarine slices per serving)*

SERVE WITH

1 pound fresh asparagus (about 20 spears), cooked 2 minutes, cooled under cold water, and served as a salad bed

Calories 20; total fat 0g (saturated fat 0g); protein 2g; carbohydrates 4g; fiber 2g; cholesterol 0mg; sodium 0mg; vitamin A 15%; vitamin C 10%; calcium 2%; iron 10%

2 medium nectarines or peaches, pitted and sliced (2 cups)

Calories 35; total fat 0g (saturated fat 0g); protein 1g; carbohydrates 8g; fiber 1g; cholesterol 0mg; sodium 0mg; vitamin A 2%; vitamin C 8%; calcium 0%; iron 2%

Mozzarella and Bean Salad

with Tortilla Chips, Sour Cream, and Baby Carrots

Calories 350; total fat 12g (saturated fat 4.5g); protein 16g; carbohydrates 47g; fiber 8g; cholesterol 20mg; sodium 1,020mg; vitamin A 180%; vitamin C 80%; calcium 35%; iron 15%

1½ cups (8 ounces) sweet grape tomatoes, halved

1 15-ounce can black beans, rinsed and drained

4 ounces mozzarella cheese, cut into ¼-inch cubes

½ medium green bell pepper, chopped fine (½ cup)

⅓ cup finely chopped onion

¼ cup chopped fresh cilantro

3 tablespoons fat-free Italian salad dressing

2 tablespoons lime juice or to taste

⅛ teaspoon salt

▶ Combine all the ingredients in a medium bowl and toss gently yet thoroughly until well blended. Add more lime juice, if desired.

Calories 170; total fat 7g (saturated fat 3.5g); protein 12g; carbohydrates 17g; fiber 5g; cholesterol 15mg; sodium 670mg; vitamin A 15%; vitamin C 70%; calcium 25%; iron 10%

TIME-SHAVER TIP: *To save time, use reduced-fat cheese "crumbles" instead of cutting the cheese into small cubes.*

Excellent source of fiber, vitamins A and C, and calcium

Good source of iron

Makes 4 cups salad total

Serves 4 *(1 cup salad, 1 ounce chips, 2 tablespoons sour cream, and 6 baby carrots per serving)*

SERVE WITH

4 ounces low-fat tortilla chips and ½ cup fat-free sour cream

Calories 160; total fat 4.5g (saturated fat 1g); protein 4g; carbohydrates 26g; fiber 2g; cholesterol 5mg; sodium 310mg; vitamin A 4%; vitamin C 0%; calcium 10%; iron 2%

½ pound baby carrots (about 24 total)

Calories 20; total fat 0g (saturated fat 0g); protein 0g; carbohydrates 5g; fiber 1g; cholesterol 0mg; sodium 45mg; vitamin A 160%; vitamin C 8%; calcium 2%; iron 2%

Chef's Chopped Salad

with Cracked Pepper Water Crackers, Sharp Cheddar Cheese, and Fresh Strawberries

Calories 350; total fat 10g (saturated fat 5g); protein 22g; carbohydrates 44g; fiber 8g; cholesterol 140mg; sodium 1,040mg; vitamin A 60%; vitamin C 160%; calcium 30%; iron 15%

2 slices reduced-calorie whole-wheat bread, cut into ½-inch cubes

½ cup fat-free ranch dressing

2 medium garlic cloves, minced

5 cups packed chopped romaine lettuce

¾ cup (3 ounces) turkey ham, sliced thin and chopped

½ medium cucumber, peeled and chopped (1 cup)

½ cup frozen green peas, thawed

4 large hard-boiled eggs, 2 yolks discarded, chopped

Makes about 8 cups salad total

Serves 4 *(about 2 cups salad, 5 crackers, 1 ounce cheese, and 1 cup berries per serving)*

► Preheat the oven to 350°F.

► Place the bread cubes on a cookie sheet in a single layer and bake 8 minutes or until lightly golden. Cool completely.

► Meanwhile, in a small bowl, stir together the ranch dressing and garlic; set aside.

► Combine the lettuce, ham, cucumber, and peas in a large bowl. Add the salad dressing mixture and toss gently yet thoroughly to coat completely. Add the bread cubes and chopped egg; toss gently.

Calories 170; total fat 4g (saturated fat 1g); protein 12g; carbohydrates 21g; fiber 4g; cholesterol 120mg; sodium 710mg; vitamin A 50%; vitamin C 20%; calcium 6%; iron 10%

SERVE WITH

20 cracked pepper water crackers and 4 ounces reduced-fat sharp cheddar cheese, sliced thin

Calories 130; total fat 6g (saturated fat 4g); protein 8g; carbohydrates 11g; fiber 1g; cholesterol 20mg; sodium 330mg; vitamin A 6%; vitamin C 0%; calcium 20%; iron 2%

4 cups fresh whole strawberries

Calories 45; total fat 0g (saturated fat 0g); protein 1g; carbohydrates 11g; fiber 3g; cholesterol 0mg; sodium 0mg; vitamin A 0%; vitamin C 140%; calcium 2%; iron 4%

> **TIME-SHAVER TIP:** *When a recipe calls for minced fresh garlic, reach for a garlic press. They're easy to use and easy to clean, and you don't have to pull out a cutting board.*

Excellent source of fiber, vitamins A and C, and calcium

Good source of iron

Chicken–Goat Cheese Spinach Salad and Raspberry Dressing

with Fresh Strawberries and Cinnamon Crisps

Calories 350; total fat 12g (saturated fat 4g); protein 23g; carbohydrates 39g; fiber 5g; cholesterol 50mg; sodium 310mg; vitamin A 35%; vitamin C 80%; calcium 15%; iron 20%

¾ cup fat-free raspberry salad dressing

2 teaspoons grated gingerroot or grated orange rind

6 cups (12 ounces) packed baby spinach

1½ cups (½ pound) cooked diced chicken breast

½ medium red onion, sliced thin (½ cup)

2 ounces goat cheese, cut into small pieces

¼ cup (1 ounce) sliced almonds, toasted

▶ Combine the salad dressing and ginger in a small bowl; whisk until well blended. Place the spinach on the bottom of a serving platter or four individual dinner plates, and top with the chicken and onion. Spoon the dressing evenly over all and top with the cheese and almonds.

Calories 250; total fat 9g (saturated fat 3.5g); protein 21g; carbohydrates 21g; fiber 3g; cholesterol 50mg; sodium 240mg; vitamin A 35%; vitamin C 15%; calcium 10%; iron 15%

COOK'S NOTE: *The addition of ginger or orange rind gives an extra punch of fresh flavor to this popular salad.*

Excellent source of fiber, vitamins A and C, and iron

Good source of calcium

Makes about 12 cups salad total

Serves 4 (about 3 cups salad, ½ cup berries, and 5 crisps per serving)

SERVE WITH

2 cups quartered strawberries

Calories 25; total fat 0g (saturated fat 0g); protein 0g; carbohydrates 6g; fiber 1g; cholesterol 0mg; sodium 0mg; vitamin A 0%; vitamin C 70%; calcium 2%; iron 2%

20 cinnamon cracker crisps

Calories 80; total fat 2.5g (saturated fat 0.5g); protein 1g; carbohydrates 13g; fiber 1g; cholesterol 0mg; sodium 70mg; vitamin A 0%; vitamin C 0%; calcium 2%; iron 4%

Flash-Fix Crunchy Tortilla Rounds

with Celery and Frozen Sweet Grapes

Calories 350; total fat 10g (saturated fat 4.5g); protein 22g; carbohydrates 49g; fiber 6g; cholesterol 50mg; sodium 600mg; vitamin A 15%; vitamin C 35%; calcium 30%; iron 10%

8 soft soft corn tortillas

½ pound extra-lean ground beef

½ teaspoon salt

½ teaspoon ground cumin

¾ cup (3 ounces) reduced-fat sharp cheddar cheese, shredded

2 medium jalapeño peppers, seeded and chopped fine

1 medium tomato, seeded and chopped (1 cup)

½ cup fat-free sour cream

¼ cup chopped fresh cilantro, optional

▶ Line an oven rack with foil and preheat the oven to 425°F.

▶ Place the tortillas on the foil, and bake 9 minutes or until beginning to brown lightly.

▶ Meanwhile, cook the beef with the salt and cumin in a large nonstick skillet over medium-high heat.

▶ Remove the tortillas from the oven, and top with the cheese, pepper, beef mixture, and tomato. Return to the oven, turn the oven off, and let stand until cheese melts, about 2 minutes.

▶ Top with the sour cream and cilantro.

Calories 280; total fat 9g (saturated fat 4.5g); protein 21g; carbohydrates 30g; fiber 4g; cholesterol 50mg; sodium 550mg; vitamin A 15%; vitamin C 10%; calcium 25%; iron 10%

COOK'S NOTE: Be sure to place the tortillas on foil or they will burn.

Excellent source of fiber, vitamin C, and calcium

Good source of vitamin A and iron

Makes 8 tortilla rounds total

Serves 4 (2 tortilla rounds, 3 celery pieces, and 1 cup grapes per serving)

SERVE WITH

4 medium celery stalks, trimmed and cut into 3 pieces each

Calories 10; total fat 0g (saturated fat 0g); protein 1g; carbohydrates 2g; fiber 1g; cholesterol 0mg; sodium 50mg; vitamin A 2%; vitamin C 8%; calcium 2%; iron 2%

4 cups frozen seedless green or red grapes

Calories 60; total fat 0.5g (saturated fat 0g); protein 1g; carbohydrates 16g; fiber 1g; cholesterol 0mg; sodium 0mg; vitamin A 2%; vitamin C 15%; calcium 2%; iron 2%

Salsa Verde Pork Tortilla Flats

with Diced Mango

Calories 350; total fat 7g (saturated fat 2.5g); protein 30g; carbohydrates 46g; fiber 4g; cholesterol 75mg; sodium 520mg; vitamin A 25%; vitamin C 60%; calcium 10%; iron 10%

4 boneless pork chops, trimmed of fat (1 pound total)

½ teaspoon ground cumin

¼ teaspoon salt

4 medium green onions, chopped coarse (about ¾ cup)

4 whole-wheat flour tortillas, warmed

2 cups shredded lettuce

½ cup salsa verde

½ cup fat-free sour cream

¼ cup chopped fresh cilantro, optional

1 medium lime, quartered

▶ Sprinkle one side of the pork with the cumin and salt; set aside on a separate plate.

▶ Heat a large nonstick skillet over medium-high heat until hot, and coat the skillet with cooking spray. Add the pork and cook 4 minutes on each side or until barely pink in the center;

place on a cutting board. Coat any pan residue in the skillet with cooking spray. Add the onion in a single layer, coat it with cooking spray, cook 2 minutes, turn, and cook another 2 minutes or until beginning to brown. Set aside on the cutting board. Slice the pork into thin strips.

▶ To assemble, place the tortillas on four individual dinner plates and top each with equal amounts (in order) of lettuce, salsa verde, sour cream, cilantro, and pork. Squeeze lime juice evenly over all and top with green onions. Serve open face.

Calories 280; total fat 7g (saturated fat 2.5g); protein 30g; carbohydrates 29g; fiber 3g; cholesterol 75mg; sodium 510mg; vitamin A 10%; vitamin C 8%; calcium 10%; iron 10%

COOK'S NOTE: *Salsa verde is green salsa made from tomatillos, green chilies, and cilantro and can be found where picante sauce and other salsas are sold.*

Excellent source of vitamins A and C

Good source of fiber, calcium, and iron

Makes 4 tortilla flats total

Serves 4 *(1 tortilla flat and ½ cup mango per serving)*

SERVE WITH

2 medium mangoes, peeled and diced (2 cups)

Calories 70; total fat 0g (saturated fat 0g); protein 1g; carbohydrates 18g; fiber 2g; cholesterol 0mg; sodium 0mg; vitamin A 15%; vitamin C 50%; calcium 2%; iron 0%

So Sloppy Turkey Joes

with Corn on the Cob and Celery Stalks

Calories 350; total fat 6g (saturated fat 0g); protein 31g; carbohydrates 52g; fiber 8g; cholesterol 35mg; sodium 980mg; vitamin A 15%; vitamin C 70%; calcium 8%; iron 20%

¾ **pound 99% fat-free ground turkey breast**

1 **14.5-ounce can diced tomatoes with onions and peppers, reserving liquid**

2 **teaspoons Worcestershire sauce**

2 **tablespoons ketchup**

1 **cup frozen green bell peppers, thawed**

1 **teaspoon beef bouillon granules**

4 **whole-wheat hamburger buns, lightly toasted**

▶ Heat a large nonstick skillet over medium-high heat until hot, and coat the skillet with cooking spray. Add the turkey and cook until no longer pink, stirring constantly. Add the remaining ingredients except the buns, reduce heat, cover, and simmer 10 minutes, stirring occasionally.

▶ If time allows, let stand 15 minutes to absorb flavors before serving.

▶ Spoon equal amounts on each of the buns.

Calories 250; total fat 3.5g (saturated fat 0g); protein 26g; carbohydrates 33g; fiber 5g; cholesterol 35mg; sodium 930mg; vitamin A 10%; vitamin C 50%; calcium 6%; iron 15%

Excellent source of fiber, vitamin C, and iron

Good source of vitamin A

Makes 4 sandwiches total

Serves 4 *(1 sandwich, 1 ear of corn, and 3 celery pieces per serving)*

SERVE WITH

4 medium ears of corn, boiled

> Calories 90; total fat 2.5g (saturated fat 0g); protein 4g; carbohydrates 16g; fiber 2g; cholesterol 0mg; sodium 0mg; vitamin A 2%; vitamin C 10%; calcium 0%; iron 2%

4 medium celery stalks, trimmed and cut into 3 pieces each

> Calories 10; total fat 0g (saturated fat 0g); protein 1g; carbohydrates 2g; fiber 1g; cholesterol 0mg; sodium 50mg; vitamin A 2%; vitamin C 8%; calcium 2%; iron 2%

Smoked Sausage Fryers

with Speed-Baked Sweet Potato Halves

Calories 350; total fat 6g (saturated fat 1.5g); protein 15g; carbohydrates 60g; fiber 8g; cholesterol 25mg; sodium 900mg; vitamin A 440%; vitamin C 90%; calcium 15%; iron 15%

10 ounces smoked turkey sausage

1 medium green bell pepper, chopped (1 cup)

1 medium yellow onion, chopped (1 cup)

¼ cup water

4 whole-wheat hot dog buns, lightly toasted

1 tablespoon plus 1 teaspoon honey mustard

▶ Cut the sausage in half lengthwise. Cut each sausage half in half crosswise, creating four pieces total.

▶ Heat a large nonstick skillet over medium-high heat until hot, and coat the skillet with cooking spray. Add the bell pepper and onion, coat them with cooking spray, and cook 8 minutes or until richly browned, stirring frequently. Add the water and cook 30 seconds or until almost evaporated. Place in a small bowl, cover with foil, and set aside.

▶ Coat the skillet with cooking spray and heat over medium-high heat. Add the sausage and cook 4 minutes or until browned, stirring frequently.

▶ To serve, place a piece of sausage on each of the buns, spoon 1 teaspoon of the honey mustard on each, and top with the pepper mixture.

Calories 240; total fat 4g (saturated fat 1g); protein 13g; carbohydrates 36g; fiber 4g; cholesterol 25mg; sodium 830mg; vitamin A 2%; vitamin C 60%; calcium 8%; iron 10%

TIME-SHAVER TIP: *The pepper mixture is placed in a small bowl and covered so that it can retain the heat, continue cooking without drying out, and at the same time absorb the smokiness that was created from browning the vegetables in the skillet.*

Excellent source of fiber and vitamins A and C

Good source of calcium and iron

Makes 4 sandwiches total

Serves 4 *(1 sandwich, ½ sweet potato, and 1 teaspoon margarine per serving)*

SERVE WITH

2 medium sweet potatoes (12 ounces), pierced, cooked in the microwave on High for 6 to 8 minutes until tender, halved, and topped with 4 teaspoons diet margarine

Calories 120; total fat 1.5g (saturated fat 0g); protein 2g; carbohydrates 24g; fiber 4g; cholesterol 0mg; sodium 70mg; vitamin A 440%; vitamin C 35%; calcium 4%; iron 4%

Ground Beef and Sausage Burgers

with Fresh Broccoli and Cucumber Rounds with Dipping Sauce

Calories 350; total fat 11g (saturated fat 3.5g); protein 28g; carbohydrates 38g; fiber 5g; cholesterol 65mg; sodium 860mg; vitamin A 30%; vitamin C 50%; calcium 10%; iron 15%

¾ pound extra-lean ground beef

¼ pound 50% less-fat bulk pork sausage, such as Jimmy Dean

3 tablespoons steak sauce, such as A.1.

½ teaspoon salt-free steak grilling blend, such as Mrs. Dash

4 whole-wheat hamburger buns

4 teaspoons ketchup

4 thin red onion slices

4 romaine or red lettuce leaves

▶ Preheat the broiler.

▶ Combine the ground beef, sausage, and steak sauce in a medium bowl, being careful not to overwork the meat. Shape into four patties and sprinkle evenly with the grilling blend. Place on a broiler rack and pan, and broil at least 4 inches from heat source, 5 minutes on each side. Remove from the broiler.

▶ Place the cut side of buns under the broiler, watching closely so they do not burn. Place the beef patties on the buns with ketchup, onion, and lettuce.

Calories 300; total fat 11g (saturated fat 3.5g); protein 25g; carbohydrates 27g; fiber 4g; cholesterol 65mg; sodium 670mg; vitamin A 10%; vitamin C 4%; calcium 6%; iron 15%

Makes 4 burgers total

Serves 4 *(1 burger, about ⅔ cup raw vegetables, and 2 tablespoons dipping sauce per serving)*

SERVE WITH

1½ cups broccoli florets and ½ medium cucumber, peeled and sliced (1 cup), with ¼ cup fat-free creamy salad dressing mixed with ¼ cup fat-free sour cream

Calories 50; total fat 0g (saturated fat 0g); protein 2g; carbohydrates 10g; fiber 1g; cholesterol 0mg; sodium 200mg; vitamin A 20%; vitamin C 45%; calcium 4%; iron 2%

COOK'S NOTE: *The small amount of pork sausage imparts a subtle yet hearty flavor to the burgers. This also helps to add seasoning without using a lot of ingredients.*

Excellent source of fiber and vitamins A and C

Good source of calcium and iron

Easy Provolone, Basil, and Kalamata Paninis

with Red Bell Pepper Strips, Star Fruit, and Frozen Fruit Pops

Calories 350; total fat 10g (saturated fat 3g); protein 13g; carbohydrates 51g; fiber 7g; cholesterol 10mg; sodium 890mg; vitamin A 80%; vitamin C 360%; calcium 25%; iron 15%

8 ounces sourdough or Tuscan-style bread, cut into 8 slices

2 tablespoons plus 2 teaspoons fat-free Italian salad dressing

4 1-ounce slices reduced-fat provolone cheese

4 medium plum tomatoes, sliced (2 cups)

16 fresh basil leaves

1 cup (2 ounces) packed baby spinach or regular spinach, chopped coarse

16 pitted kalamata olives, chopped

▶ Lightly spray one side of each of the bread slices with cooking spray. Turn the slices over and spoon 1 teaspoon of the salad dressing on each. Top four bread slices with a cheese slice and equal amounts of the tomato, basil, spinach, and olives. Top with the other four bread slices, salad dressing side down.

▶ Heat a large nonstick skillet over medium heat until hot, and coat the skillet with cooking spray. Add the sandwiches and cook 1½ to 2 minutes or until lightly golden, turn, and reduce heat to medium low. (Add weight to the sandwiches by covering them with a sheet of foil and topping with a dinner plate and a couple of cans of soup or vegetables.) Cook 2 minutes or until browned on the bottom. Remove from heat and let stand, covered, 2 minutes.

Calories 270; total fat 9g (saturated fat 3g); protein 11g; carbohydrates 35g; fiber 3g; cholesterol 10mg; sodium 880mg; vitamin A 25%; vitamin C 15%; calcium 20%; iron 10%

Excellent source of fiber, vitamins A and C, and calcium

Good source of iron

Makes 4 sandwiches total

Serves 4 *(1 sandwich, ½ cup bell pepper slices, 1 cup star fruit slices, and 2 fruit pops per serving)*

SERVE WITH

2 medium red bell peppers, cut into thin strips (2 cups)

Calories 20; total fat 0g (saturated fat 0g); protein 1g; carbohydrates 5g; fiber 2g; cholesterol 0mg; sodium 0mg; vitamin A 50%; vitamin C 270%; calcium 0%; iron 2%

4 medium star fruit, sliced (4 cups)

Calories 30; total fat 0g (saturated fat 0g); protein 1g; carbohydrates 6g; fiber 3g; cholesterol 0mg; sodium 0mg; vitamin A 2%; vitamin C 50%; calcium 0%; iron 0%

8 sugar-free frozen fruit pops

Calories 35; total fat 0g (saturated fat 0g); protein 0g; carbohydrates 6g; fiber 0g; cholesterol 0mg; sodium 5mg; vitamin A 0%; vitamin C 20%; calcium 0%; iron 0%

Spring Greens and Swiss Chicken on English Muffins

with Cinnamon-Sugared Apple Slices

Calories 350; total fat 8g (saturated fat 2.5g); protein 37g; carbohydrates 31g; fiber 4g; cholesterol 80mg; sodium 480mg; vitamin A 10%; vitamin C 15%; calcium 25%; iron 8%

¼ cup honey mustard

1½ tablespoons diet mayonnaise

4 boneless, skinless chicken breast halves (1 pound total), flattened to ¼-inch thickness

Freshly ground black pepper to taste

¼ teaspoon salt

4 1-ounce slices reduced-fat Swiss cheese

2 whole-wheat English muffins, halved

¼ cup thinly sliced red onion

2 cups (4 ounces) packed spring greens

▶ Combine the mustard and mayonnaise in a small bowl and set aside.

▶ Sprinkle both sides of the chicken pieces with the pepper and salt. Heat a nonstick skillet over medium-high heat until hot, and coat the skillet with cooking spray. Cook the chicken 2 to 3 minutes on each side or until no longer pink in the center. Remove from heat, top each chicken piece with a cheese slice, cover, and let stand 1 minute to allow the cheese to melt slightly.

► Meanwhile, toast the muffins and spread equal amounts of the mustard mixture on each muffin half. Top the muffin halves with equal amounts of the onion and greens. Top each with the chicken and cheese.

Calories 310; total fat 8g (saturated fat 2.5g); protein 37g; carbohydrates 19g; fiber 2g; cholesterol 80mg; sodium 480mg; vitamin A 10%; vitamin C 8%; calcium 25%; iron 8%

TIME-SHAVER TIP: *To flatten chicken quickly, place all four pieces on a large sheet of plastic wrap, cover with another sheet, and use a meat mallet or the bottom of a heavy bottle to pound to a ¼-inch thickness. This makes for easy cleanup too!*

Excellent source of calcium

Good source of fiber and vitamins A and C

Makes 4 open-face sandwiches total

Serves 4 *(1 sandwich, ¾ cup apple slices, and ½ teaspoon cinnamon sugar per serving)*

SERVE WITH

3 medium apples, sliced (3 cups), sprinkled with
2 teaspoons cinnamon sugar

Calories 45; total fat 0g (saturated fat 0g); protein 0g; carbohydrates 12g; fiber 1g; cholesterol 0mg; sodium 0mg; vitamin A 0%; vitamin C 6%; calcium 0%; iron 0%

99

Grilled Ham, Onion, and Rye

with Baked Potato Chips, Celery Sticks, and Watermelon

Calories 350; total fat 7g (saturated fat 2.5g); protein 20g; carbohydrates 59g; fiber 9g; cholesterol 25mg; sodium 820mg; vitamin A 30%; vitamin C 60%; calcium 30%; iron 15%

8 slices reduced-calorie rye bread

2 tablespoons plus 2 teaspoons dijonnaise

4 1-ounce slices reduced-fat Swiss cheese

¼ pound turkey ham, sliced thin

8 medium green onions (white part only), chopped fine (½ cup)

▶ Lightly spray one side of each of the bread slices with cooking spray. Turn the slices over and spoon 1 teaspoon of the dijonnaise on each. Top four bread slices with a cheese slice and equal amounts of the turkey and onion. Top with the other four bread slices, dijonnaise side down.

▶ Heat a large nonstick skillet over medium heat until hot, and coat skillet with cooking spray. Add the sandwiches and cook 3 minutes or until golden brown. Coat the bread with cooking spray, turn, and cook 2 to 3 minutes or until browned on the bottom.

▶ Remove from heat and let stand, covered, 2 minutes.

Calories 190; total fat 6g (saturated fat 2.5g); protein 16g; carbohydrates 22g; fiber 6g; cholesterol 25mg; sodium 580mg; vitamin A 6%; vitamin C 4%; calcium 25%; iron 10%

TIME-SHAVER TIP: *Turkey ham is often sold in one piece or sliced. If you buy it in one piece, have the butcher slice it thin for you. When you get home, separate it into smaller quantities and store it in small freezer bags. Pop them into the freezer and pull them out as you need them.*

Excellent source of fiber, vitamins A and C, and calcium

Good source of iron

Makes 4 sandwiches total

Serves 4 *(1 sandwich, 1 ounce chips, 3 celery pieces, and 1½ cups watermelon cubes per serving)*

SERVE WITH

4 ounces baked fat-free potato chips

Calories 80; total fat 0g (saturated fat 0g); protein 2g; carbohydrates 17g; fiber 1g; cholesterol 0mg; sodium 180mg; vitamin A 0%; vitamin C 15%; calcium 0%; iron 2%

4 medium celery stalks, trimmed and cut into 3 pieces each

Calories 10; total fat 0g (saturated fat 0g); protein 1g; carbohydrates 2g; fiber 1g; cholesterol 0mg; sodium 50mg; vitamin A 2%; vitamin C 8%; calcium 2%; iron 2%

6 cups watermelon cubes

Calories 70; total fat 0g (saturated fat 0g); protein 1g; carbohydrates 17g; fiber 1g; cholesterol 0mg; sodium 0mg; vitamin A 25%; vitamin C 30%; calcium 2%; iron 4%

Country Herbed-Cheese Crostini

with Grapefruit Sections and Baby Carrots

Calories 350; total fat 7g (saturated fat 3.5g); protein 15g; carbohydrates 59g; fiber 6g; cholesterol 35mg; sodium 920mg; vitamin A 360%; vitamin C 130%; calcium 20%; iron 20%

8 ounces French country bread or sourdough bread, cut in 4 slices

½ cup (4 ounces) light garlic and herb cream cheese spread, such as Alouette

16 small fresh basil leaves

1 medium tomato, sliced thin (1 cup)

2 cups (4 ounces) packed spring greens

¼ pound oven-roasted deli turkey, sliced thin

▶ Place the bread slices on a baking sheet and place in a cold oven. Set the oven for 350°F. Turn the bread after 4 minutes. When the oven reaches 350°F (about 8 minutes total), turn it off, remove the bread, and cool completely.

▶ Top each slice with equal amounts of (in order) the cheese spread, basil, tomato slices, greens, and turkey. Serve open face; cut in half, if desired.

Calories 260; total fat 7g (saturated fat 3.5g); protein 13g; carbohydrates 35g; fiber 2g; cholesterol 35mg; sodium 830mg; vitamin A 20%; vitamin C 15%; calcium 15%; iron 10%

Makes 4 open-face sandwiches total

Serves 4 (1 sandwich, ¾ cup grapefruit sections, and about 10 baby carrots per serving)

SERVE WITH

3 cups pink grapefruit sections

Calories 60; total fat 0g (saturated fat 0g); protein 1g; carbohydrates 14g; fiber 2g; cholesterol 0mg; sodium 0mg; vitamin A 30%; vitamin C 100%; calcium 2%; iron 0%

1 pound baby carrots (about 40 total)

Calories 40; total fat 0g (saturated fat 0g); protein 1g; carbohydrates 9g; fiber 2g; cholesterol 0mg; sodium 90mg; vitamin A 310%; vitamin C 15%; calcium 4%; iron 4%

TIME-SHAVER TIP: *Placing the bread in the oven while it is heating allows the bread to "slow toast," making it crispy without overbrowning or having to wait the extra minutes for the oven to heat up.*

Excellent source of fiber, vitamins A and C, calcium, and iron

Lemon Vinaigrette Greens on Italian Bread

with Sweet Grape Tomatoes and Pineapple Spears

Calories 350; total fat 11g (saturated fat 2g); protein 11g; carbohydrates 53g; fiber 7g; cholesterol 0mg; sodium 580mg; vitamin A 25%; vitamin C 35%; calcium 10%; iron 20%

6 ounces Italian bread, cut into 8 slices, lightly toasted, and cooled

2 medium garlic cloves, halved crosswise

4 cups (8 ounces) packed spring greens

1 15.5-ounce can navy beans, rinsed and drained

¼ cup finely chopped red onion

2 tablespoons chopped fresh basil

2 tablespoons plus 2 teaspoons extra-virgin olive oil

1 tablespoon plus 1 teaspoon lemon juice or cider vinegar

▶ Rub the toasted bread lightly with garlic. Top each serving with equal amounts of the greens, beans, onion, and basil. Spoon 2 teaspoons of the oil and 1 teaspoon of the lemon juice over each serving.

Calories 290; total fat 11g (saturated fat 2g); protein 10g; carbohydrates 38g; fiber 6g; cholesterol 0mg; sodium 570mg; vitamin A 15%; vitamin C 10%; calcium 8%; iron 15%

COOK'S TIP: Don't skip the garlic-rubbing step. The garlic provides an extra layer of flavor.

Excellent source of fiber, vitamins A and C, and iron

Good source of calcium

Makes 8 open-face sandwiches total

Serves 4 *(2 sandwiches, ½ cup sweet grape tomatoes, and 3 pineapple spears per serving)*

SERVE WITH

2 cups sweet grape tomatoes (10 ounces)

Calories 15; total fat 0g (saturated fat 0g); protein 1g; carbohydrates 3g; fiber 1g; cholesterol 0mg; sodium 0mg; vitamin A 10%; vitamin C 15%; calcium 0%; iron 2%

12 canned pineapple spears

Calories 45; total fat 0g (saturated fat 0g); protein 0g; carbohydrates 12g; fiber 1g; cholesterol 0mg; sodium 0mg; vitamin A 0%; vitamin C 10%; calcium 2%; iron 2%

Avocado, Feta, and Sprout Pitas

with Clam Chowder and Blueberry-Honeydew Cups

Calories 350; total fat 11g (saturated fat 3.5g); protein 18g; carbohydrates 51g; fiber 9g; cholesterol 20mg; sodium 1,360mg; vitamin A 15%; vitamin C 60%; calcium 15%; iron 15%

1 cup (8 ounces) nonfat plain yogurt

¼ cup finely chopped red onion

1 teaspoon dried dill weed

¼ teaspoon salt

½ medium cucumber, peeled and chopped (1 cup)

1 ripe medium avocado, peeled, seeded, and chopped (1 cup)

1 cup (4 ounces) crumbled reduced-fat feta

2 whole-wheat pitas, halved and warmed

2 cups (4 ounces) alfalfa sprouts or packed spring greens

▶ Stir together the yogurt, onion, dill, and salt in a small bowl and set aside. Combine the cucumber, avocado, and feta in another small bowl and toss gently.

▶ To assemble, fill each pita half with equal amounts of the sprouts, top with the cucumber mixture, and spoon the yogurt mixture evenly over all.

Calories 200; total fat 9g (saturated fat 3g); protein 12g; carbohydrates 23g; fiber 5g; cholesterol 10mg; sodium 670mg; vitamin A 15%; vitamin C 15%; calcium 15%; iron 6%

TIME-SHAVER TIP: There's a wide variety of reduced-fat, reduced-sodium soups on the market now. Keep them on hand, in your pantry or even in your desk drawer, to fall back on when a cup of hot soup is needed (and to save you from a fast-food line).

Excellent source of fiber and vitamin C

Good source of vitamin A, calcium, and iron

Makes 4 stuffed pita halves total

Serves 4 *(1 pita half, about ¾ cup soup, 1 cup diced honeydew, and ¼ cup blueberries per serving)*

SERVE WITH

3 cups reduced-fat clam chowder

Calories 80; total fat 1g (saturated fat 0g); protein 5g; carbohydrates 11g; fiber 2g; cholesterol 10mg; sodium 670mg; vitamin A 2%; vitamin C 0%; calcium 0%; iron 6%

4 cups diced honeydew sprinkled with 1 cup fresh blueberries

Calories 70; total fat 0g (saturated fat 0g); protein 1g; carbohydrates 17g; fiber 2g; cholesterol 0mg; sodium 25mg; vitamin A 2%; vitamin C 45%; calcium 0%; iron 2%

Chicken-Almond Hoisin Wraps

with Scallioned Soup, Sesame Seed Rice Crackers, and Dried Apricots

Calories 350; total fat 12g (saturated fat 1g); protein 19g; carbohydrates 42g; fiber 6g; cholesterol 30mg; sodium 900mg; vitamin A 70%; vitamin C 150%; calcium 10%; iron 15%

3 tablespoons hoisin sauce

½ teaspoon grated orange rind

⅓ cup orange juice

⅛ teaspoon dried pepper flakes

3 cups shredded coleslaw with carrots

1 medium red bell pepper, chopped (1 cup)

1 cup (5 ounces) cooked diced chicken breast

¾ cup (3 ounces) slivered almonds, toasted

12 Boston or Bibb or green-leaf lettuce leaves

▶ Stir together the hoisin sauce, orange rind, juice, and pepper flakes in a small bowl and set aside.

▶ Combine the coleslaw, bell pepper, chicken, and almonds in a medium bowl and toss to blend. Drizzle filling with hoisin mixture. Spoon equal amounts into each of the 12 lettuce leaves and wrap.

Calories 240; total fat 12g (saturated fat 1g); protein 17g; carbohydrates 18g; fiber 4g; cholesterol 30mg; sodium 450mg; vitamin A 50%; vitamin C 150%; calcium 10%; iron 10%

COOK'S NOTE: Be sure to use slivered almonds, not the sliced variety, in this recipe for a definitely crunchy texture.

TIME-SHAVER TIP: This is fun to serve when entertaining. Fill the wraps, but place them open on a large serving platter so everyone can wrap up their own.

Excellent source of fiber and vitamins A and C

Good source of calcium and iron

Makes 12 wraps total

Serves 4 (3 wraps, about ¾ cup soup, 6 crackers, and 6 apricot halves per serving)

SERVE WITH

3 cups reduced-sodium chicken broth, heated and mixed with 4 medium green onions, chopped (½ cup), and 1 teaspoon light soy sauce

Calories 10; total fat 0g (saturated fat 0g); protein 1g; carbohydrates 1g; fiber 1g; cholesterol 0mg; sodium 390mg; vitamin A 2%; vitamin C 4%; calcium 2%; iron 0%

24 sesame seed rice wafer crackers

Calories 45; total fat 0g (saturated fat 0g); protein 1g; carbohydrates 9g; fiber 0g; cholesterol 0mg; sodium 60mg; vitamin A 0%; vitamin C 0%; calcium 0%; iron 0%

24 dried apricot halves

Calories 50; total fat 0g (saturated fat 0g); protein 1g; carbohydrates 13g; fiber 2g; cholesterol 0mg; sodium 0mg; vitamin A 15%; vitamin C 0%; calcium 2%; iron 4%

Unwrapped Roast Beef and Blue Cheese Wraps

with Balsamic-Splashed Beet Slices and Fresh Orange Sections

Calories 350; total fat 6g (saturated fat 3g); protein 22g; carbohydrates 60g; fiber 9g; cholesterol 40mg; sodium 910mg; vitamin A 80%; vitamin C 190%; calcium 25%; iron 15%

½ cup fat-free sour cream

3 tablespoons dijonnaise

4 whole-wheat flour tortillas, warmed

4 cups (8 ounces) packed romaine lettuce, chopped coarse

½ medium red onion, chopped fine (½ cup)

½ pound deli roast beef, sliced thin

1 cup alfalfa sprouts

½ cup (2 ounces) blue cheese, crumbled

▶ Combine the sour cream and dijonnaise in a small bowl and spread equal amounts on each of the four tortillas. Top with equal amounts of the lettuce, onion, beef, and sprouts; sprinkle cheese evenly over all. Serve open face.

Calories 240; total fat 6g (saturated fat 3g); protein 19g; carbohydrates 32g; fiber 3g; cholesterol 40mg; sodium 870mg; vitamin A 70%; vitamin C 25%; calcium 15%; iron 10%

COOK'S NOTE: *This makes a beautiful open-face salad wrap! A knife and fork works best. No need for rolling; you'll miss out on the layers of flavors if you do.*

Excellent source of fiber, vitamins A and C, and calcium

Good source of iron

Makes 4 sandwiches total

Serves 4 *(1 sandwich, ⅓ cup sliced beets, about ½ teaspoon vinegar, and 1 cup orange sections per serving)*

SERVE WITH

1⅓ cups sliced canned or jarred beets sprinkled with 2 to 3 teaspoons balsamic vinegar

Calories 25; total fat 0g (saturated fat 0g); protein 1g; carbohydrates 6g; fiber 1g; cholesterol 0mg; sodium 45mg; vitamin A 0%; vitamin C 4%; calcium 0%; iron 2%

4 cups orange sections

Calories 80; total fat 0g (saturated fat 0g); protein 2g; carbohydrates 21g; fiber 4g; cholesterol 0mg; sodium 0mg; vitamin A 8%; vitamin C 160%; calcium 8%; iron 2%

105

Hummus, Swiss, and Rye Crispbreads

with Shredded Cabbage–Balsamic Salad and Fresh Plums

Calories 340; total fat 12g (saturated fat 3g); protein 15g; carbohydrates 50g; fiber 10g; cholesterol 10mg; sodium 700mg; vitamin A 15%; vitamin C 70%; calcium 25%; iron 15%

¾ **cup prepared hummus**

12 rye crispbreads, such as Wasa

4 ¾-ounce slices reduced-fat Swiss cheese, cut in 3 strips each

3 medium plum tomatoes, sliced thin (1½ cups)

12 pitted kalamata olives, chopped fine

▶ Spoon 1 tablespoon of the hummus on each of the crispbreads, top with ⅓ cheese slice and equal amounts of the tomato slices and olives.

Calories 270; total fat 12g (saturated fat 3g); protein 13g; carbohydrates 31g; fiber 8g; cholesterol 10mg; sodium 460mg; vitamin A 10%; vitamin C 10%; calcium 25%; iron 10%

COOK'S NOTE: *Prepared hummus (generally made from chickpeas) is sold in a wide variety of flavors and can be found near the specialty cheese section in your supermarket. Some may have more fat and sodium than others, so read the labels and compare.*

Excellent source of fiber, vitamin C, and calcium

Good source of vitamin A and iron

Makes 12 crispbreads total

Serves 4 *(3 crispbreads, 1 cup salad, 1 tablespoon vinegar, and 1 plum per serving)*

SERVE WITH

4 cups shredded coleslaw mix topped with ¼ cup balsamic salad dressing

Calories 35; total fat 0g (saturated fat 0g); protein 1g; carbohydrates 8g; fiber 2g; cholesterol 0mg; sodium 240mg; vitamin A 2%; vitamin C 60%; calcium 4%; iron 2%

4 medium plums

Calories 40; total fat 0g (saturated fat 0g); protein 1g; carbohydrates 11g; fiber 1g; cholesterol 0mg; sodium 0mg; vitamin A 4%; vitamin C 6%; calcium 0%; iron 2%

4

Dinners

SEAFOOD

▸ Fish Fillets in Chunky Creole Sauce

▸ Buttery Toasted-Almond Fish Fillets

▸ Fish Fillets and Creamy Lemon-Dijon Sauce

▸ Roasted Salmon and Fresh Pineapple Salsa

▸ Shrimp, Sausage, and Bayou Rice

▸ Black Pepper–Lemon Shrimp

POULTRY

▸ Oregano Chicken and Capers

▸ Buttermilk-Battered Fried Chicken Tenders

▸ Spicy Lemon-Mustard Chicken

▸ Creamy Herbed Chicken and Noodles

▸ Chipotle Chicken-and-Rice Skillet Casserole

▸ Garlic Chicken and Bok Choy

▸ Double Cheese–Stuffed Turkey Patties

▸ Pepperoni-Basil Pasta

BEEF

▸ Beef Tenderloin and Sweet Marsala Mushrooms

▸ Sirloin Steak and Sweet Bourbon Reduction

▸ Skillet Meatloaf Rounds

▸ French-Onion Beef and Carrots

▸ Mexican Green-Chili Skillet Casserole

PORK

▸ Thyme-Rubbed Skillet Pork Chops

▸ Seared Pork Tenderloin and Horseradish-Rosemary Aioli

▸ Spiced Pork and Dark Cherry–Ginger Salsa

▸ Pork Chops and Tarragon-Lemon Rice

▸ Speedy Chimichurri-Style Pork Chops

▸ Fresh Ginger–Pork Potsticker Bowls

MEATLESS

▸ Stuffed Quick-Baked Potatoes, Cheese Sauce, and Broccoli

▸ Feta, Edamame, and Fresh Herb Penne

▸ Skillet Rice and Black Beans

▸ Skillet Garden au Gratin

▸ Pinto Bean Shepherd's Pie

Fish Fillets in Chunky Creole Sauce

with Corn-and-Zucchini Toss and Creamy Country Coleslaw

Calories 350; total fat 11g (saturated fat 2g); protein 30g; carbohydrates 40g; fiber 6g; cholesterol 50mg; sodium 650mg; vitamin A 25%; vitamin C 140%; calcium 10%; iron 10%

1 medium celery stalk, sliced thin (½ cup)

½ medium yellow onion, chopped fine (½ cup)

½ medium green bell pepper, chopped fine (½ cup)

1 cup (5 ounces) sweet grape tomatoes, quartered

2 tablespoons diet margarine

2 tablespoons chopped fresh parsley

½ teaspoon Louisiana hot sauce or to taste

4 snapper fillets or other lean white fish fillets (1 pound total)

½ teaspoon salt

▶ Heat a large nonstick skillet over medium heat until hot, and coat the skillet with cooking spray. Add the celery, onion, and bell pepper; coat them with cooking spray; and cook 6 minutes or until just beginning to brown lightly. Add the tomato and margarine; cook 30 seconds. Stir in the parsley and hot sauce. Place in a small bowl, cover, and set aside.

▶ Recoat the skillet with cooking spray and place over medium-high heat. Sprinkle the fillets evenly with ¼ teaspoon of the salt and cook 3 minutes; turn and cook 2 minutes or until opaque in the center. Remove from heat. Stir the remaining ¼ teaspoon salt into the tomato mixture and pour over the fish fillets. Cover and let stand 2 minutes to heat slightly and absorb flavors.

Calories 160; total fat 4g (saturated fat 1g); protein 24g; carbohydrates 5g; fiber 1g; cholesterol 40mg; sodium 420mg; vitamin A 20%; vitamin C 45%; calcium 6%; iron 4%

COOK'S NOTE: *Be sure to use the sweet grape variety of tomatoes for peak flavor and texture.*

Excellent source of fiber and vitamins A and C

Good source of calcium and iron

Makes 4 fillets and 1½ cups sauce total

Serves 4 *(3 ounces cooked fish, rounded ⅓ cup sauce, 1 cup corn mixture, 1 cup coleslaw, and 1 tablespoon dressing per serving)*

SERVE WITH

3 cups frozen corn (1 pound) steamed with 1 medium zucchini, diced (1 cup)

Calories 120; total fat 1g (saturated fat 0g); protein 5g; carbohydrates 27g; fiber 3g; cholesterol 0mg; sodium 0mg; vitamin A 6%; vitamin C 35%; calcium 2%; iron 4%

4 cups coleslaw mix tossed with ¼ cup coleslaw dressing

Calories 80; total fat 6g (saturated fat 1g); protein 1g; carbohydrates 7g; fiber 2g; cholesterol 10mg; sodium 220mg; vitamin A 2%; vitamin C 60%; calcium 4%; iron 2%

Buttery Toasted-Almond Fish Fillets

with Fresh Ginger Rice, Steamed Sugar Snaps, and Apricot Halves

Calories 350; total fat 12g (saturated fat 2g); protein 28g; carbohydrates 34g; fiber 4g; cholesterol 75mg; sodium 310mg; vitamin A 30%; vitamin C 30%; calcium 6%; iron 15%

½ cup (2 ounces) sliced almonds

1½ tablespoons diet margarine

1 teaspoon Worcestershire sauce

½ teaspoon grated lemon rind

¼ plus ⅛ teaspoon salt

4 tilapia fillets or other lean white fish fillets (1 pound total)

½ teaspoon paprika

2 tablespoons water

1 tablespoon lemon juice

▶ Heat a large nonstick skillet over medium-high heat until hot. Add the almonds and cook 2 to 3 minutes or until beginning to brown lightly, stirring frequently. Remove from heat, and stir in the margarine, Worcestershire sauce, lemon rind, and ¼ teaspoon of the salt; set aside in a separate bowl.

▶ Sprinkle both sides of the fish evenly with the paprika and remaining ⅛ teaspoon salt. Heat the skillet over medium heat, add the fish, coat it with cooking spray, and cook 3 to 4 minutes on each side or until opaque in the center. Place the fish on a serving platter.

▶ Stir the water and lemon juice into the almond mixture, and spoon evenly over the fish.

Calories 210; total fat 11g (saturated fat 2g); protein 25g; carbohydrates 3g; fiber 1g; cholesterol 75mg; sodium 300mg; vitamin A 4%; vitamin C 2%; calcium 4%; iron 6%

TIME-SHAVER TIP: *Double or triple the amount of almonds toasted and store in ¼-cup quantities in small plastic bags to keep on hand. Toasting nuts brings out their flavor without adding extra fat grams.*

Excellent source of vitamins A and C

Good source of fiber and iron

Makes 4 fillets and ½ cup almond mixture total

Serves 4 *(3 ounces cooked fish, 2 tablespoons almond mixture, ½ cup rice, ½ cup sugar snap peas, and ½ cup apricot halves per serving)*

SERVE WITH

2 cups cooked brown rice tossed with ½ teaspoon grated gingerroot and 1 tablespoon chopped cilantro (or green onion)

Calories 60; total fat 0.5g (saturated fat 0g); protein 2g; carbohydrates 13g; fiber 1g; cholesterol 0mg; sodium 0mg; vitamin A 0%; vitamin C 0%; calcium 0%; iron 0%

2 cups sugar snap peas, steamed (10 ounces)

Calories 25; total fat 0g (saturated fat 0g); protein 1g; carbohydrates 4g; fiber 1g; cholesterol 0mg; sodium 0mg; vitamin A 2%; vitamin C 20%; calcium 2%; iron 6%

1 16-ounce can apricot halves, drained (2 cups)

Calories 50; total fat 0g (saturated fat 0g); protein 0g; carbohydrates 14g; fiber 1g; cholesterol 0mg; sodium 10mg; vitamin A 25%; vitamin C 8%; calcium 0%; iron 2%

Fish Fillets and Creamy Lemon-Dijon Sauce

with New Potatoes, Sugar Snaps, and Romaine-Crouton Salad

Calories 350; total fat 12g (saturated fat 2.5g); protein 29g; carbohydrates 33g; fiber 6g; cholesterol 80mg; sodium 690mg; vitamin A 50%; vitamin C 100%; calcium 10%; iron 20%

2 medium lemons, sliced

4 fish fillets, such as tilapia, rinsed and patted dry
   (1 pound total)

Freshly ground black pepper to taste

2 tablespoons light mayonnaise

⅓ cup fat-free yogurt

½ teaspoon dried dill weed

1 teaspoon Dijon mustard

1 teaspoon lemon juice

6 to 8 drops hot pepper sauce or to taste

⅛ teaspoon salt

► Preheat the oven to 400°F.

► Place the lemon slices in a single layer on the bottom of a
13″ × 9″ baking pan. Arrange the fillets on top. Sprinkle with
black pepper, cover, and bake 18 minutes or until opaque in
the center.

▶ Meanwhile, combine the remaining ingredients in a small saucepan and cook over medium-low heat until just warmed, stirring frequently. Do not bring to a boil. Place the fish on a serving platter and spoon sauce evenly over all. Sprinkle with additional black pepper and serve with additional lemon wedges.

Calories 150; total fat 5g (saturated fat 1g); protein 23g; carbohydrates 3g; fiber 0g; cholesterol 80mg; sodium 210mg; vitamin A 2%; vitamin C 4%; calcium 2%; iron 2%

COOK'S NOTE: *With the wide varieties of croutons on the market, it's easy to get confused. Look for the fat-free variety and those with the lowest sodium content and the highest amount of fiber.*

Excellent source of fiber, vitamins A and C, and iron

Good source of calcium

Makes 4 fillets plus ½ cup sauce total

Serves 4 *(3 ounces cooked fish, 2 tablespoons sauce, 4 ounces potatoes, about ½ cup peas, 2 cups salad, 2 tablespoons dressing, and 2 tablespoons croutons per serving)*

SERVE WITH

1 pound new potatoes, boiled

Calories 70; total fat 0g (saturated fat 0g); protein 3g; carbohydrates 15g; fiber 2g; cholesterol 0mg; sodium 0mg; vitamin A 0%; vitamin C 45%; calcium 0%; iron 4%

2 cups sugar snap peas (10 ounces), steamed and tossed with 1 tablespoon diet margarine

Calories 40; total fat 1g (saturated fat 0g); protein 2g; carbohydrates 5g; fiber 2g; cholesterol 0mg; sodium 25mg; vitamin A 4%; vitamin C 25%; calcium 4%; iron 8%

1 10-ounce package (5 cups packed) torn romaine lettuce tossed with ½ cup reduced-fat salad dressing and ½ cup fat-free croutons

Calories 90; total fat 5g (saturated fat 1g); protein 2g; carbohydrates 10g; fiber 2g; cholesterol 0mg; sodium 460mg; vitamin A 45%; vitamin C 20%; calcium 4%; iron 6%

Roasted Salmon and Fresh Pineapple Salsa

with Sautéed Red Pepper and Black Beans with Lime, and Warm Corn Tortillas

Calories 350; total fat 14g (saturated fat 2.5g); protein 28g; carbohydrates 28g; fiber 7g; cholesterol 65mg; sodium 440mg; vitamin A 20%; vitamin C 120%; calcium 6%; iron 15%

4 salmon fillets, skinned, rinsed, and patted dry (1 pound total)

2 medium garlic cloves, halved crosswise

½ teaspoon dried thyme leaves

¼ teaspoon salt

1 cup finely chopped fresh pineapple

1 jalapeño pepper, seeded and chopped fine, or dried pepper flakes

2 tablespoons finely chopped red onion

2 tablespoons chopped mint

1 teaspoon grated gingerroot

▶ Preheat the oven to 350°F.

▶ Rub both sides of the fillets evenly with the garlic halves, and place the fish on a foil-lined baking sheet. Sprinkle evenly with the thyme and salt; bake 20 minutes or until opaque in the center.

▶ Meanwhile, in a small bowl, combine the remaining ingredients and let stand 10 minutes to allow flavors to blend. Serve alongside the salmon.

Calories 230; total fat 12g (saturated fat 2.5g); protein 23g; carbohydrates 6g; fiber 1g; cholesterol 65mg; sodium 210mg; vitamin A 2%; vitamin C 35%; calcium 2%; iron 4%

🥄 **TIME-SHAVER TIP:** Be sure to line the baking sheet with foil. It saves time on cleanup and prevents sticking.

Excellent source of fiber and vitamins A and C

Good source of iron

Makes 4 fillets and 1 cup fruit salsa total

Serves 4 *(3 ounces cooked fish, ¼ cup salsa, ½ cup bean mixture, and 1 tortilla per serving)*

SERVE WITH

1 medium red pepper, sliced (1 cup), sautéed, tossed with 1 15-ounce can rinsed black beans, and drizzled with the juice of 1 medium lime

Calories 70; total fat 0.5g (saturated fat 0g); protein 4g; carbohydrates 12g; fiber 4g; cholesterol 0mg; sodium 220mg; vitamin A 20%; vitamin C 90%; calcium 2%; iron 8%

4 soft soft corn tortillas, warmed

Calories 60; total fat 0.5g (saturated fat 0g); protein 1g; carbohydrates 12g; fiber 2g; cholesterol 0mg; sodium 10mg; vitamin A 0%; vitamin C 0%; calcium 2%; iron 2%

Shrimp, Sausage, and Bayou Rice

with Steamed Broccoli, Red Wine Vinaigrette on Shredded Cabbage, and Fresh Garlic-Rubbed French Bread Slices

Calories 350; total fat 4.5g (saturated fat 1g); protein 25g; carbohydrates 53g; fiber 6g; cholesterol 100mg; sodium 1,080mg; vitamin A 60%; vitamin C 200%; calcium 15%; iron 20%

12 ounces frozen pepper stir-fry

1½ cups water

6 ounces smoked turkey sausage, sliced thin

1 cup dry quick-cooking brown rice

½ pound raw shrimp, peeled

½ cup chipotle or medium picante sauce

¾ to 1 teaspoon sugar

Louisiana hot sauce to taste

> Combine the pepper stir-fry and water in a blender and puree until smooth; set aside.

> Heat a large skillet over medium-high heat until hot, and coat the skillet with cooking spray. Add the sausage, coat it with cooking spray, and cook 5 minutes or until browned, stirring frequently. Set aside on a separate plate. Add the pureed mixture and rice to the pan residue; stir until the brown residue is released from the bottom of the skillet. Bring to a boil over medium-high heat; reduce heat, cover, and simmer 12 minutes or until the liquid is absorbed.

> Stir in the shrimp, chipotle, and sausage; cook 5 minutes or until the shrimp are opaque in the center, stirring occasionally. Remove from heat, stir in the sugar, and let stand 5 minutes to absorb flavors. Serve with hot sauce.

Calories 230; total fat 3g (saturated fat 0.5g); protein 20g; carbohydrates 29g; fiber 2g; cholesterol 100mg; sodium 690mg; vitamin A 10%; vitamin C 30%; calcium 4%; iron 10%

COOK'S NOTE: The sugar added does not make the dish sweeter, but it softens the flavors to help them blend together without adding more fat.

Excellent source of fiber, vitamins A and C, and iron

Good source of calcium

Makes 5 cups sausage mixture total

Serves 4 *(1¼ cups sausage mixture, 1 cup broccoli, 1 cup cabbage salad, 1 tablesppon vinaigrette, and 1 slice bread per serving)*

SERVE WITH

4 cups broccoli florets, steamed (10 ounces)

Calories 20; total fat 0g (saturated fat 0g); protein 2g; carbohydrates 4g; fiber 2g; cholesterol 0mg; sodium 20mg; vitamin A 45%; vitamin C 110%; calcium 4%; iron 4%

4 cups shredded cabbage tossed with ¼ cup fat-free red wine vinegar salad dressing

Calories 25; total fat 0g (saturated fat 0g); protein 1g; carbohydrates 5g; fiber 2g; cholesterol 0mg; sodium 220mg; vitamin A 2%; vitamin C 60%; calcium 4%; iron 2%

4 ounces French bread, cut into 4 slices, lightly toasted, and rubbed with fresh garlic halves

Calories 70; total fat 1g (saturated fat 1g); protein 2g; carbohydrates 15g; fiber 1g; cholesterol 0mg; sodium 150mg; vitamin A 0%; vitamin C 0%; calcium 4%; iron 4%

113

Black Pepper–Lemon Shrimp

with Tender New Potatoes, Asparagus Spears, and Tomatoes with Creamy Onion Topping

Calories 350; total fat 7g (saturated fat 1.5g); protein 35g; carbohydrates 35g; fiber 6g; cholesterol 215mg; sodium 590mg; vitamin A 40%; vitamin C 90%; calcium 15%; iron 30%

2 teaspoons grated lemon rind

¼ cup lemon juice

3 medium garlic cloves, minced

1 teaspoon seafood seasoning, such as Old Bay

½ teaspoon coarsely ground black pepper

⅛ teaspoon cayenne, optional

1¼ pounds raw shrimp, peeled, rinsed, and patted dry

1 to 1½ teaspoons Worcestershire sauce

¼ cup diet margarine

2 tablespoons chopped fresh parsley

▶ Preheat the oven to 425°F.

▶ Combine the lemon rind, lemon juice, garlic, seafood seasoning, black pepper, and cayenne in a small bowl and stir until well blended.

▶ Place the shrimp in a 13″ × 9″ baking pan in a single layer; pour the lemon mixture evenly over all. Bake 8 minutes or until the shrimp are opaque in the center. Pour the pan drippings into a small saucepan with the Worcestershire sauce. Bring to a boil over high heat and boil 30 to 45 seconds or until slightly reduced. Remove from heat, stir in the margarine until just melted, and spoon over the shrimp. Sprinkle evenly with the parsley.

Calories 200; total fat 7g (saturated fat 1.5g); protein 29g; carbohydrates 4g; fiber 0g; cholesterol 215mg; sodium 480mg; vitamin A 15%; vitamin C 15%; calcium 8%; iron 20%

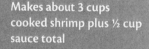 **COOK'S NOTE:** *You can serve the shrimp mixture as is or spoon it over the asparagus and potatoes.*

Excellent source of fiber, vitamins A and C, and iron

Good source of calcium

Makes about 3 cups cooked shrimp plus ½ cup sauce total

Serves 4 *(¾ cup shrimp, 2 tablespoons sauce, 4 ounces potatoes, 4 ounces asparagus, 3 to 4 tomato slices, and about 2 tablespoons dressing per serving)*

SERVE WITH

1 pound new potatoes, boiled

Calories 80; total fat 0g (saturated fat 0g); protein 2g; carbohydrates 18g; fiber 2g; cholesterol 0mg; sodium 5mg; vitamin A 0%; vitamin C 35%; calcium 2%; iron 4%

1 pound asparagus (about 20 spears), steamed

Calories 30; total fat 0g (saturated fat 0g); protein 2g; carbohydrates 5g; fiber 2g; cholesterol 0mg; sodium 0mg; vitamin A 10%; vitamin C 20%; calcium 2%; iron 2%

3 medium tomatoes (3 cups), sliced and topped with 2 tablespoons fat-free creamy dressing and sour cream, and ¼ cup chopped green onions

Calories 35; total fat 0g (saturated fat 0g); protein 1g; carbohydrates 8g; fiber 1g; cholesterol 0mg; sodium 100mg; vitamin A 15%; vitamin C 20%; calcium 2%; iron 2%

Oregano Chicken and Capers

with New Potatoes and Steamed Asparagus Spears

Calories 350; total fat 9g (saturated fat 1.5g); protein 32g; carbohydrates 33g; fiber 6g; cholesterol 65mg; sodium 360mg; vitamin A 25%; vitamin C 80%; calcium 6%; iron 25%

¼ cup dry white wine, such as chardonnay

2 tablespoons capers, drained

2 medium garlic cloves, minced

1½ teaspoons lemon juice

¼ teaspoon salt

⅛ teaspoon black pepper

4 4-ounce boneless, skinless chicken breast halves, flattened to ¼-inch thickness

2 teaspoons dried oregano leaves

2 tablespoons extra-virgin olive oil

¼ cup chopped fresh parsley

▶ Combine the wine, capers, garlic, lemon juice, salt, and pepper in a small bowl and set aside.

▶ Sprinkle both sides of the chicken evenly with the oregano. Heat a large nonstick skillet over medium-high heat until hot, and coat the skillet with cooking spray. Cook the chicken 2 to 3 minutes on each side or until no longer pink in the center. Do not overcook. Place on a serving platter.

▶ Add the wine mixture to the skillet and boil 30 seconds, scraping the bottom and sides of the skillet. Remove from heat, stir in the oil, and pour evenly over the chicken pieces. Sprinkle evenly with the parsley.

Calories 200; total fat 8g (saturated fat 1.5g); protein 26g; carbohydrates 1g; fiber 0g; cholesterol 65mg; sodium 350mg; vitamin A 6%; vitamin C 15%; calcium 2%; iron 6%

Excellent source of fiber, vitamins A and C, and iron

Makes 4 chicken breast halves with ¼ cup sauce total

Serves 4 (3 ounces cooked chicken, 1 tablespoon sauce, 6 ounces potatoes, and 4 ounces asparagus per serving)

SERVE WITH

1½ pounds small new potatoes, boiled

Calories 120; total fat 0g (saturated fat 0g); protein 3g; carbohydrates 27g; fiber 3g; cholesterol 0mg; sodium 10mg; vitamin A 0%; vitamin C 60%; calcium 2%; iron 6%

1 pound asparagus (about 20 spears), steamed, and 1 medium lemon, quartered

Calories 25; total fat 0g (saturated fat 0g); protein 2g; carbohydrates 4g; fiber 2g; cholesterol 0mg; sodium 0mg; vitamin A 15%; vitamin C 10%; calcium 2%; iron 15%

Buttermilk-Battered Fried Chicken Tenders

with Faux Mashed Potatoes and Steamed Green Peas

Calories 350; total fat 11g (saturated fat 1g); protein 35g; carbohydrates 31g; fiber 8g; cholesterol 70mg; sodium 500mg; vitamin A 36%; vitamin C 120%; calcium 8%; iron 18%

½ cup fat-free buttermilk

8 chicken tenders, rinsed and patted dry (about 1 pound total)

½ cup all-purpose flour

¼ teaspoon paprika

¼ teaspoon garlic powder

¼ teaspoon black pepper

½ teaspoon salt

2 tablespoons canola oil

▶ Pour the buttermilk into a medium bowl, add the chicken, and toss to coat completely.

▶ Place the flour, paprika, garlic powder, black pepper, and all but ⅛ teaspoon of the salt in a shallow pan, such as a pie pan, and stir until well blended.

▶ Working with two tenders at a time, remove from the buttermilk, coat with the flour mixture, and set aside on a separate plate. Continue until all tenders are coated. Sprinkle any remaining flour mixture evenly over all.

▶ Heat a large nonstick skillet and the oil over medium-high heat until hot. Add the chicken and immediately reduce heat to medium. Cook 6 minutes on each side or until golden and no longer pink in the center. Sprinkle with the remaining ⅛ teaspoon salt.

Calories 230; total fat 8g (saturated fat 0.5g); protein 28g; carbohydrates 12g; fiber 0g; cholesterol 70mg; sodium 360mg; vitamin A 0%; vitamin C 0%; calcium 2%; iron 8%

*✎ **TIME-SHAVER TIP:** The chicken is even better the next day, so it makes a great brown-bag lunch for kids of all ages.*

Excellent source of fiber, vitamins A and C, and iron

Makes 12 ounces cooked chicken total

Serves 4 *(3 ounces cooked chicken, about ¾ cup cauliflower mixture, ½ cup peas, and 2 cucumber spears per serving)*

SERVE WITH

2 10-ounce packages frozen cauliflower, steamed and pureed in a blender with 2 tablespoons diet margarine

Calories 60; total fat 2.5g (saturated fat 0.5g); protein 3g; carbohydrates 8g; fiber 4g; cholesterol 0mg; sodium 90mg; vitamin A 6%; vitamin C 110%; calcium 4%; iron 4%

2 cups frozen green peas, steamed (10 ounces)

Calories 60; total fat 0g (saturated fat 0g); protein 4g; carbohydrates 10g; fiber 4g; cholesterol 0mg; sodium 50mg; vitamin A 30%; vitamin C 10%; calcium 2%; iron 6%

Spicy Lemon-Mustard Chicken

with Pimiento Rice and Steamed Fresh Spinach

Calories 350; total fat 9g (saturated fat 1.5g); protein 44g; carbohydrates 24g; fiber 5g; cholesterol 100mg; sodium 610mg; vitamin A 70%; vitamin C 45%; calcium 10%; iron 25%

2 tablespoons Dijon mustard

1 teaspoon grated lemon rind

1 tablespoon lemon juice

2 tablespoons capers, drained

1 tablespoon extra-virgin olive oil

1 teaspoon dried oregano leaves

¼ teaspoon hot pepper sauce

4 6-ounce boneless, skinless chicken breast halves, rinsed and patted dry

2 tablespoons water

2 tablespoons chopped fresh parsley

► Combine the mustard, lemon rind, lemon juice, capers, olive oil, oregano, and hot pepper sauce in a small bowl. Using a fork or the back of a spoon, mash the capers to release the juices; stir and set aside.

► Heat a large nonstick skillet over medium-high heat until hot, and coat the skillet with cooking spray. Add the chicken and cook 4 minutes; turn and top with the mustard mixture. Reduce heat to medium low, cover tightly, and cook 15 minutes or until no longer pink in the center.

▶ Remove from heat, scrape the sauce from the chicken into the skillet, and place the chicken on a serving platter. Add the water to the sauce, scraping the bottom and sides of the skillet, and cook 1 minute. Pour evenly over the chicken and sprinkle with parsley.

Calories 230; total fat 6g (saturated fat 1g); protein 40g; carbohydrates 1g; fiber 0g; cholesterol 100mg; sodium 430mg; vitamin A 0%; vitamin C 6%; calcium 4%; iron 8%

COOK'S NOTE: *Mashing the capers is a great way to disperse their flavor without adding too much sodium to the dish.*

Excellent source of fiber, vitamins A and C, and iron

Good source of calcium

Makes 4 chicken breast halves plus ½ cup sauce total

Serves 4 *(4½ ounces cooked chicken, 2 tablespoons sauce, ½ cup rice mixture, about ½ cup cooked spinach, and 1½ teaspoons margarine per serving)*

SERVE WITH

2 cups cooked brown rice tossed with 1 2-ounce jar diced pimiento

Calories 70; total fat 0.5g (saturated fat 0g); protein 2g; carbohydrates 13g; fiber 1g; cholesterol 0mg; sodium 5mg; vitamin A 8%; vitamin C 20%; calcium 0%; iron 2%

2 6-ounce packages fresh baby spinach, steamed and seasoned with 2 tablespoons diet margarine

Calories 60; total fat 2g (saturated fat 0g); protein 2g; carbohydrates 10g; fiber 4g; cholesterol 0mg; sodium 180mg; vitamin A 70%; vitamin C 20%; calcium 6%; iron 15%

Creamy Herbed Chicken and Noodles

with Mixed Greens, Artichoke, and Sweet Grape Tomato Salad

Calories 350; total fat 8g (saturated fat 4g); protein 25g; carbohydrates 45g; fiber 3g; cholesterol 55mg; sodium 850mg; vitamin A 40%; vitamin C 35%; calcium 20%; iron 20%

6 ounces dry no-yolk egg noodles

½ pound boneless, skinless chicken breast, cut into bite-size pieces

½ teaspoon salt

½ cup (4 ounces) light cream cheese with herbs and garlic, such as Alouette

2 tablespoons fat-free milk

1 medium garlic clove, minced

3 medium green onions, chopped fine (⅓ cup)

1 tablespoon grated Parmesan cheese

▶ Cook the noodles according to the package directions, omitting any salt or fat.

▶ Meanwhile, heat a medium skillet over medium heat until hot, and coat the skillet with cooking spray. Cook the chicken 4 minutes or until no longer pink in the center, stirring frequently.

▶ Drain the noodles, return them to the pot, and add the chicken and remaining ingredients, except the Parmesan cheese. Toss until the cream cheese has melted and the mixture is well blended. Sprinkle with the Parmesan.

Calories 290; total fat 6g (saturated fat 4g); protein 22g; carbohydrates 36g; fiber 2g; cholesterol 55mg; sodium 530mg; vitamin A 2%; vitamin C 4%; calcium 15%; iron 10%

TIME-SHAVER TIP: *To save time, you can use about 1¼ cups cooked chicken in place of the raw chicken, using either leftovers from a rotisserie chicken or the frozen chopped variety.*

Excellent source of vitamins A and C, calcium, and iron

Good source of fiber

Makes 5 cups chicken-and-noodle mixture total

Serves 4 *(1¼ cups chicken-and-noodle mixture and about 1¾ cups salad per serving)*

SERVE WITH

4 cups mixed greens topped with 1 14-ounce can quartered artichoke hearts, drained; 1¼ cups sweet grape tomatoes; and 40 sprays Caesar-flavored salad spritzer

Calories 60; total fat 1g (saturated fat 0g); protein 3g; carbohydrates 9g; fiber 2g; cholesterol 0mg; sodium 320mg; vitamin A 40%; vitamin C 30%; calcium 4%; iron 10%

Chipotle Chicken-and-Rice Skillet Casserole

with Yellow Squash Stir-Fry and Pineapple-Mango Salad

Calories 350; total fat 5g (saturated fat 2g); protein 28g; carbohydrates 49g; fiber 7g; cholesterol 55mg; sodium 650mg; vitamin A 40%; vitamin C 130%; calcium 21%; iron 10%

¾ pound boneless, skinless chicken breast, cut into bite-size pieces

1½ medium yellow onions, chopped (1½ cups)

¾ cup dry quick-cooking brown rice

1¼ cups water

½ cup mild picante sauce

½ cup chopped roasted red peppers

1 chipotle chili pepper, minced, plus 1 tablespoon of the adobo sauce (the sauce in which the chipotle is packed)

⅛ to ¼ teaspoon salt

½ cup (2 ounces) shredded mozzarella cheese

▶ Heat a medium nonstick skillet over medium-high heat until hot, and coat the skillet with cooking spray. Add the chicken and cook 2 minutes, stirring constantly. (The chicken will still be pink in the center at this point.) Set aside on a separate plate.

▶ Recoat the skillet with cooking spray. Add the onion, coat it with cooking spray, and cook 4 minutes or until translucent, stirring frequently. Add the rice, water, picante sauce, peppers, and chicken. Bring to a boil, reduce heat, cover, and simmer 14 minutes or until the water is almost absorbed. Remove from heat and stir in the salt. Sprinkle evenly with the cheese, and let stand 2 minutes to allow the cheese to melt slightly.

Calories 240; total fat 5g (saturated fat 2g); protein 26g; carbohydrates 23g; fiber 3g; cholesterol 55mg; sodium 640mg; vitamin A 30%; vitamin C 35%; calcium 15%; iron 6%

🥄 **COOK'S NOTE:** *Chipotle chilies are smoked jalapeños. They are sold in a can and packed with a tomatoey adobo sauce. Using the sauce is a great way to season the dish without too much chopping.*

Excellent source of fiber, vitamins A and C, and calcium

Good source of iron

Makes 5 cups chicken-and-rice mixture total

Serves 4 *(1¼ cups chicken-and-rice mixture, about ⅔ cup squash mixture, and about ¾ cup fruit per serving)*

SERVE WITH

3 medium yellow squashes, sliced (3 cups), and ½ large yellow onion, chopped (¾ cup), cooked quickly with cooking spray

Calories 35; total fat 0g (saturated fat 0g); protein 1g; carbohydrates 8g; fiber 3g; cholesterol 0mg; sodium 0mg; vitamin A 4%; vitamin C 20%; calcium 4%; iron 4%

2 cups diced fresh pineapple mixed with 1 medium mango, cubed (1 cup), and drizzled with the juice of 1 medium lime

Calories 70; total fat 0g (saturated fat 0g); protein 1g; carbohydrates 19g; fiber 2g; cholesterol 0mg; sodium 0mg; vitamin A 8%; vitamin C 70%; calcium 2%; iron 2%

121

Garlic Chicken and Bok Choy

with Snow Peas, Green-Onion Rice, and Ginger Vinaigrette Slaw

Calories 340; total fat 6g (saturated fat 1g); protein 27g; carbohydrates 43g; fiber 6g; cholesterol 50mg; sodium 740mg; vitamin A 90%; vitamin C 130%; calcium 10%; iron 15%

¾ pound boneless, skinless chicken breast, cut into ¼-inch thick strips

2 cups sliced bok choy (about 4 stalks, trimmed)

1 medium onion, cut into 8 wedges and layers separated (4 ounces)

1 medium carrot, peeled and sliced thin diagonally (⅔ cup)

4 medium garlic cloves, minced

1 cup 99% fat-free chicken broth

2 teaspoons cornstarch

2 tablespoons light soy sauce

⅛ teaspoon salt

▶ Heat a large nonstick skillet over medium-high heat until hot, and coat the skillet with cooking spray. Add the chicken and cook 3 minutes, stirring with two utensils constantly. (The chicken will still be pink in the center at this point.) Set aside on a separate plate.

▶ Recoat the skillet with cooking spray. Add the bok choy, onion, carrot, garlic, and ¼ cup of the broth; bring to a boil over medium-high heat, cover, and cook (on medium high) 4 minutes or until the vegetables are tender crisp.

▶ Meanwhile, combine the remaining ¾ cup broth with the remaining ingredients, and whisk until the cornstarch is completely dissolved.

▶ Remove the cover from the skillet, and cook 1 minute or until the liquid has evaporated. Add the chicken, any accumulated juices, and the broth mixture. Bring to a boil and cook 1 minute, stirring frequently.

Calories 130; total fat 1.5g (saturated fat 0g); protein 21g; carbohydrates 8g; fiber 1g; cholesterol 50mg; sodium 590mg; vitamin A 80%; vitamin C 35%; calcium 6%; iron 6%

TIME-SHAVER TIP: *This is a very fast-cooking dish, so be sure to have everything ready before you begin.*

Excellent source of fiber and vitamins A and C

Good source of calcium and iron

Makes 4 cups chicken-and-vegetable mixture total

Serves 4 *(1 cup chicken-and-vegetable mixture, ¾ cup snow peas, ½ cup rice, 1 cup coleslaw, and 1 tablespoon vinaigrette per serving)*

SERVE WITH

1 6-ounce package frozen snow peas (about 3 cups), steamed, to serve as a bed for the stir-fry

Calories 20; total fat 0g (saturated fat 0g); protein 1g; carbohydrates 3g; fiber 1g; cholesterol 0mg; sodium 0mg; vitamin A 2%; vitamin C 35%; calcium 2%; iron 4%

2 cups quick-cooked brown rice tossed with ¼ cup chopped green onion (about 2 medium)

Calories 130; total fat 1g (saturated fat 0g); protein 3g; carbohydrates 26g; fiber 2g; cholesterol 0mg; sodium 10mg; vitamin A 0%; vitamin C 2%; calcium 0%; iron 2%

4 cups coleslaw mix tossed with ¼ cup light ginger vinaigrette

Calories 50; total fat 3.5g (saturated fat 0.5g); protein 1g; carbohydrates 5g; fiber 2g; cholesterol 0mg; sodium 135mg; vitamin A 2%; vitamin C 60%; calcium 4%; iron 2%

Double Cheese–Stuffed Turkey Patties

with Quick-Baked Acorn Squash and Steamed Mixed Vegetables

Calories 340; total fat 7g (saturated fat 3g); protein 43g; carbohydrates 32g; fiber 4g; cholesterol 70mg; sodium 490mg; vitamin A 116%; vitamin C 35%; calcium 20%; iron 20%

1¼ pounds 99% fat-free ground turkey breast

2 teaspoons Worcestershire sauce

¼ teaspoon salt

½ cup (2 ounces) shredded reduced-fat sharp cheddar cheese

3 tablespoons (¾ ounce) crumbled blue cheese

2 tablespoons finely chopped onion

2 tablespoons chopped fresh parsley

Paprika

▶ Preheat the broiler. Coat a foil-lined baking sheet with cooking spray and set aside.

▶ Shape the ground turkey into eight patties, and place in a single layer on the baking sheet. Sprinkle four of the patties with the Worcestershire sauce and salt.

▶ Combine the cheddar cheese, blue cheese, onion, and parsley in a small bowl, and toss gently yet thoroughly until blended. Mound equal amounts on top of the seasoned patties. Top with the remaining patties. Seal the edges by pressing them down lightly with your fingertips. Sprinkle with paprika and broil at least 4 inches from the heat source, 5 minutes on each side or until beginning to brown.

Calories 220; total fat 6g (saturated fat 3g); protein 40g; carbohydrates 2g; fiber 0g; cholesterol 70mg; sodium 450mg; vitamin A 8%; vitamin C 4%; calcium 15%; iron 10%

COOK'S NOTE: *When working with the turkey, wet your hands for easy handling.*

TIME-SHAVER TIP: *To cut squash easily, place the whole squash in the microwave on High for 2 minutes before cutting.*

Excellent source of vitamins A and C, calcium, and iron

Good source of fiber

Makes 4 patties total

Serves 4 *(1 patty, ¼ squash, ½ teaspoon honey, and about ½ cup vegetables per serving)*

SERVE WITH

1 pound acorn squash, quartered, seeded, pierced, and cooked in the microwave on High for 8 to 10 minutes until tender, and then drizzled with 2 tablespoons honey

Calories 80; total fat 0g (saturated fat 0g); protein 1g; carbohydrates 20g; fiber 2g; cholesterol 0mg; sodium 0mg; vitamin A 8%; vitamin C 20%; calcium 4%; iron 4%

2 cups frozen mixed vegetables, steamed (10 ounces)

Calories 45; total fat 0g (saturated fat 0g); protein 2g; carbohydrates 10g; fiber 2g; cholesterol 0mg; sodium 30mg; vitamin A 100%; vitamin C 10%; calcium 2%; iron 4%

Pepperoni-Basil Pasta

with Steamed Zucchini Slices and Balsamic Spring Greens Carrot Salad

Calories 340; total fat 10g (saturated fat 4.5g); protein 20g; carbohydrates 49g; fiber 10g; cholesterol 25mg; sodium 1,190mg; vitamin A 140%; vitamin C 200%; calcium 35%; iron 25%

4 ounces uncooked multigrain penne or rotini

1 cup (2 ounces) packed fresh spinach, chopped coarse

1 medium red bell pepper, chopped fine (1 cup)

1½ cups spaghetti sauce

3 tablespoons chopped fresh basil or 1 tablespoon dried basil leaves, crushed

17 small turkey pepperoni slices, quartered

1 cup (4 ounces) shredded mozzarella cheese

1 tablespoon grated Parmesan cheese

▶ Cook the pasta according to the package directions, omitting any salt or fat. Drain the pasta in a colander, add the spinach to the colander, and toss until the spinach is limp, about 30 seconds. Place in an 8-inch square baking pan. Cover to keep warm.

▶ Preheat the broiler.

▶ Coat the pasta pot with cooking spray and place over medium-high heat. Add the bell pepper and cook 1 minute, stirring constantly. Add the spaghetti sauce and cook 1 to 2 minutes or until beginning to boil; spoon sauce mixture evenly over the pasta. Sprinkle the basil and pepperoni evenly over all and top with the mozzarella cheese. Broil at least 4 inches from the heat source 1½ to 2 minutes or until beginning to turn a rich, golden brown. Remove from the broiler, sprinkle evenly with the Parmesan, and let stand 5 to 10 minutes to absorb flavors.

Calories 270; total fat 9g (saturated fat 4g); protein 16g; carbohydrates 38g; fiber 7g; cholesterol 25mg; sodium 850mg; vitamin A 45%; vitamin C 130%; calcium 25%; iron 15%

TIME-SHAVER TIP: *Tossing the spinach in the colander with the hot pasta not only lightly cooks the delicate vegetable but also saves on cleanup. The same is true for cooking the pepper and sauce in the pasta pot.*

Excellent source of fiber, vitamins A and C, calcium, and iron

Makes 1 8-inch casserole total

Serves 4 *(about 1 cup pasta mixture, about ⅓ cup zucchini, 1 cup salad, and 1 tablespoon dressing per serving)*

SERVE WITH

2 medium zucchini, sliced (2 cups) and steamed

Calories 20; total fat 0g (saturated fat 0g); protein 3g; carbohydrates 3g; fiber 1g; cholesterol 0mg; sodium 0mg; vitamin A 0%; vitamin C 60%; calcium 2%; iron 4%

3 cups mixed greens, 1 cup matchstick carrots, and 12 small ripe olives tossed with ¼ cup reduced-fat balsamic salad dressing

Calories 50; total fat 1g (saturated fat 0g); protein 1g; carbohydrates 9g; fiber 2g; cholesterol 0mg; sodium 350mg; vitamin A 100%; vitamin C 15%; calcium 4%; iron 6%

Beef Tenderloin and Sweet Marsala Mushrooms

with Fresh Garlic-Rubbed French Bread and Greens with Hearts of Palm

Calories 350; total fat 13g (saturated fat 3g); protein 28g; carbohydrates 25g; fiber 3g; cholesterol 60mg; sodium 700mg; vitamin A 30%; vitamin C 20%; calcium 10%; iron 30%

4 4-ounce beef tenderloin steaks

¼ teaspoon coarsely ground black pepper

½ teaspoon salt

2 teaspoons extra-virgin olive oil

1 8-ounce package sliced mushrooms

½ cup marsala

1 tablespoon diet margarine

¼ cup finely chopped parsley

▶ Sprinkle both sides of the beef evenly with the pepper and ¼ teaspoon of the salt. Let stand 15 minutes. Meanwhile, preheat the oven to 200°F. Heat a large nonstick skillet over medium-high heat until hot, and coat the skillet with cooking spray. Add 1 teaspoon of the oil, and tilt the skillet to coat the bottom lightly. Add the mushrooms, coat them with cooking spray, and sprinkle with the remaining ¼ teaspoon salt; cook 5 minutes or until beginning to brown, stirring frequently. Set aside on a separate plate.

▶ Return the skillet to medium-high heat, add the remaining 1 teaspoon oil, and tilt the skillet to coat the bottom. Add the beef and cook 3 minutes on each side. Reduce heat to medium low, turn the beef, and continue to cook 2 to 4 minutes or to desired doneness. Place on four dinner plates and place in the oven to keep warm.

▶ Add the marsala to the pan residue in the skillet, bring to a boil over medium-high heat, and cook 1 minute or until reduced to ¼ cup liquid. Add the mushrooms and any accumulated juices to the reduced marsala, bring to a boil, and cook 1½ minutes or until the liquid is almost evaporated. Remove from heat, add the margarine, and stir until melted. Spoon equal amounts of the mushroom sauce evenly over each steak and sprinkle each evenly with parsley.

Calories 210; total fat 8g (saturated fat 2g); protein 24g; carbohydrates 7g; fiber 0g; cholesterol 60mg; sodium 370mg; vitamin A 2%; vitamin C 2%; calcium 2%; iron 15%

TIME-SHAVER TIP: *Call the butcher before you leave for the market and have the beef prepared ahead of time so you don't have to wait.*

Excellent source of vitamins A and C and iron

Good source of fiber and calcium

Makes 4 steaks and 1 cup mushroom mixture total

Serves 4 (*3 ounces beef, ¼ cup mushroom mixture, 1¼ cups salad, 2 teaspoons dressing, and 1 slice bread per serving*)

SERVE WITH

4 cups spring greens tossed with 4 teaspoons olive oil and 4 teaspoons vinegar, topped with 1 cup canned hearts of palm, chopped

Calories 60; total fat 5g (saturated fat 0.5g); protein 2g; carbohydrates 3g; fiber 2g; cholesterol 0mg; sodium 170mg; vitamin A 30%; vitamin C 20%; calcium 6%; iron 10%

4 ounces French bread, cut into 4 slices, lightly toasted, and rubbed with fresh garlic halves

Calories 70; total fat 1g (saturated fat 0g); protein 2g; carbohydrates 15g; fiber 1g; cholesterol 0mg; sodium 150mg; vitamin A 0%; vitamin C 0%; calcium 4%; iron 4%

Sirloin Steak and Sweet Bourbon Reduction

with Quick-Baked Sweet Potatoes and Green Pepper–Yellow Squash Sauté

Calories 340; total fat 5g (saturated fat 2g); protein 28g; carbohydrates 36g; fiber 5g; cholesterol 50mg; sodium 510mg; vitamin A 330%; vitamin C 50%; calcium 8%; iron 15%

2 tablespoons light soy sauce

2 tablespoons balsamic vinegar

2 tablespoons packed dark brown sugar

1 teaspoon instant coffee granules

¼ teaspoon salt

½ teaspoon coarsely ground black pepper

1 pound boneless sirloin steak (about ¾ inch thick), trimmed of fat

¼ cup bourbon

▶ Combine the soy sauce, vinegar, sugar, coffee granules, salt, and pepper in a 13″ × 9″ baking pan. Add the sirloin, turning several times to coat. Let stand 15 minutes, turning occasionally. Meanwhile, preheat the broiler.

▶ Coat a broiler rack and pan with cooking spray, place the beef (reserving marinade) on the rack, and broil 5 minutes on each side or to desired doneness. Place on a cutting board and let stand 3 minutes before slicing thin.

▶ Pour the reserved marinade and the bourbon into a small saucepan and bring to a boil over high heat. Boil 1 to 1½ minutes or until reduced to ¼ cup. Spoon over the steak before serving.

Calories 220; total fat 4.5g (saturated fat 1.5g); protein 26g; carbohydrates 8g; fiber 0g; cholesterol 50mg; sodium 440mg; vitamin A 0%; vitamin C 0%; calcium 4%; iron 10%

COOK'S NOTE: Be sure to watch the boiling marinade closely; it reduces very quickly.

Excellent source of fiber and vitamins A and C

Good source of iron

Makes 12 ounces cooked meat and ¼ cup sauce total

Serves 4 *(3 ounces cooked meat, 1 tablespoon sauce, ½ sweet potato, plus about ½ cup vegetables per serving)*

SERVE WITH

2 medium sweet potatoes (12 ounces), pierced, cooked in the microwave on High for 10 minutes until tender, and then halved

Calories 100; total fat 0g (saturated fat 0g); protein 2g; carbohydrates 23g; fiber 3g; cholesterol 0mg; sodium 60mg; vitamin A 320%; vitamin C 4%; calcium 4%; iron 4%

1 medium green bell pepper, sliced (1 cup); 1 medium yellow squash, sliced (1 cup); and 1 medium onion, sliced (1 cup), quickly sautéed with cooking spray

Calories 20; total fat 0g (saturated fat 0g); protein 1g; carbohydrates 5g; fiber 2g; cholesterol 0mg; sodium 0mg; vitamin A 4%; vitamin C 45%; calcium 2%; iron 2%

Skillet Meatloaf Rounds

with Sautéed Zucchini and Onion, Steamed Cauliflower, and Wheat Rolls

Calories 340; total fat 7g (saturated fat 2g); protein 33g; carbohydrates 39g; fiber 9g; cholesterol 60mg; sodium 630mg; vitamin A 8%; vitamin C 170%; calcium 10%; iron 25%

1 8-ounce can tomato sauce with basil, garlic, and oregano

2 tablespoons ketchup

1 pound extra-lean ground beef

½ medium green bell pepper, chopped fine (½ cup)

½ medium onion, chopped fine (½ cup)

⅓ cup quick-cooking oats

2 large egg whites

▶ Combine the tomato sauce and ketchup in a small bowl and set aside. Combine the remaining ingredients in a medium bowl; shape into four patties.

▶ Heat a large nonstick skillet over medium-high heat until hot, and coat the skillet with cooking spray. Add the patties and cook 4 minutes or until lightly browned, turn gently, and cook 1 minute. Spoon the tomato sauce mixture over all and bring to a boil (still over medium-high heat). Reduce heat, cover, and simmer 18 minutes or until the patties are no longer pink in the center. Place the patties on a serving platter, and spoon pan drippings over all.

Calories 210; total fat 5g (saturated fat 1.5g); protein 26g; carbohydrates 14g; fiber 2g; cholesterol 60mg; sodium 460mg; vitamin A 8%; vitamin C 35%; calcium 2%; iron 15%

TIME-SHAVER TIP: These make great meatloaf sandwiches for the next day's lunch.

Excellent source of fiber, vitamin C, and iron

Good source of calcium

Makes 4 patties total

Serves 4 *(1 patty, ½ cup zucchini mixture, about ⅔ cup cauliflower, plus 1 roll per serving)*

SERVE WITH

2 medium zucchini, sliced (2 cups), and ½ medium onion, sliced (½ cup), quickly sautéed with cooking spray

Calories 25; total fat 0g (saturated fat 0g); protein 2g; carbohydrates 5g; fiber 1g; cholesterol 0mg; sodium 0mg; vitamin A 0%; vitamin C 50%; calcium 2%; iron 4%

1 pound frozen cauliflower florets, steamed

Calories 30; total fat 0g (saturated fat 0g); protein 2g; carbohydrates 6g; fiber 3g; cholesterol 0mg; sodium 35mg; vitamin A 0%; vitamin C 90%; calcium 2%; iron 2%

4 1-ounce whole-wheat dinner rolls, warmed

Calories 80; total fat 1.5g (saturated fat 0g); protein 2g; carbohydrates 14g; fiber 2g; cholesterol 0mg; sodium 135mg; vitamin A 0%; vitamin C 0%; calcium 4%; iron 4%

French-Onion Beef and Carrots

with Mashed Potatoes and Fresh Tomato Slices

Calories 350; total fat 8g (saturated fat 2.5g); protein 34g; carbohydrates 37g; fiber 4g; cholesterol 50mg; sodium 950mg; vitamin A 120%; vitamin C 35%; calcium 15%; iron 15%

¾ cup water

2 medium carrots, peeled, quartered lengthwise, and cut into 2-inch pieces (6 ounces)

1 8-ounce package whole mushrooms, quartered

1 pound boneless sirloin steak, trimmed of fat and sliced thin

1 1-ounce package dried onion soup mix

¼ cup chopped parsley

½ teaspoon coarsely ground black pepper or to taste

▶ Bring ½ cup of the water to a boil in a Dutch oven over high heat. Add the carrots and return to a boil; reduce heat, cover tightly, and simmer 3 minutes or until tender. Drain well and set aside on a plate.

▶ Place the Dutch oven over medium-high heat and coat it with cooking spray. Add the mushrooms, coat them with cooking spray, and cook 4 minutes or until tender, stirring frequently. Set aside on a separate plate.

▶ Return the Dutch oven to medium-high heat and recoat it with cooking spray. Add the beef and soup mix, and cook 2 minutes (no longer), stirring constantly. Remove from heat, add the carrots and the remaining ¼ cup water; cover and let stand 5 minutes to absorb flavors and allow juices to be released, making a gravy.

▶ Stir in the mushrooms and sprinkle with the parsley and black pepper before serving.

Calories 200; total fat 5g (saturated fat 1.5g); protein 27g; carbohydrates 11g; fiber 2g; cholesterol 50mg; sodium 710mg; vitamin A 100%; vitamin C 6%; calcium 6%; iron 15%

COOK'S NOTE: *This dish cooks quickly, so be sure to have everything measured and ready before you start.*

TIME-SHAVER TIP: *Have your butcher slice the beef thin while you finish your shopping to save even more prep and cleanup time.*

Excellent source of vitamins A and C

Good source of fiber, calcium, and iron

Makes 5 cups beef mixture total

Serves 4 *(1¼ cup beef mixture, ½ cup potatoes, and 3 to 4 tomato slices per serving)*

SERVE WITH

½ 1-pound, 6-ounce package frozen mashed potatoes, cooked according to the package directions with 1⅓ cups fat-free milk, omitting salt or fat

Calories 140; total fat 2.5g (saturated fat 0.5g); protein 6g; carbohydrates 23g; fiber 1g; cholesterol 5mg; sodium 230mg; vitamin A 6%; vitamin C 8%; calcium 8%; iron 0%

3 medium tomatoes, sliced (3 cups)

Calories 15; total fat 0g (saturated fat 0g); protein 1g; carbohydrates 3g; fiber 1g; cholesterol 0mg; sodium 0mg; vitamin A 15%; vitamin C 20%; calcium 0%; iron 2%

Mexican Green-Chili Skillet Casserole

with Green Peas, Iceberg Wedges, and Creamy Dressing

Calories 350; total fat 11g (saturated fat 3.5g); protein 21g; carbohydrates 42g; fiber 6g; cholesterol 50mg; sodium 1,240mg; vitamin A 45%; vitamin C 70%; calcium 15%; iron 20%

1⅓ cups water

¾ cup quick-cooking brown rice

⅛ teaspoon salt

½ pound extra-lean ground beef

½ large yellow onion, chopped fine (¾ cup)

½ 1.25-ounce packet taco seasoning

½ teaspoon ground cumin

½ 14.5-ounce can no-salt-added diced tomatoes, well drained

2 4.5-ounce cans chopped mild green chilies, drained

½ cup (2 ounces) shredded reduced-fat sharp cheddar cheese

▶ In a medium saucepan, bring the water and rice to a boil; reduce heat, cover tightly, and simmer 12 minutes or until the liquid is absorbed. Stir in the salt.

▶ Meanwhile, place a medium nonstick skillet over medium-high heat until hot, and coat the skillet with cooking spray. Add the beef and onion, and cook until the beef is no longer pink and the onion is translucent, stirring frequently. Remove from heat; stir in the taco seasoning and the cumin. Stir in the rice, top with the tomatoes, and arrange the chilies evenly over all. Sprinkle with the cheese, cover, and place over medium-low heat; cook 10 minutes to allow flavors to absorb and the mixture to heat thoroughly.

Calories 220; total fat 6g (saturated fat 3g); protein 17g; carbohydrates 24g; fiber 3g; cholesterol 40mg; sodium 810mg; vitamin A 10%; vitamin C 45%; calcium 15%; iron 15%

COOK'S NOTE: There's no need to use tomatoes with salt, because there is plenty of salt in the taco seasoning mix and the green chilies.

Excellent source of fiber, vitamins A and C, and iron

Good source of calcium

Makes 1 9-inch casserole total

Serves 4 (¼ casserole, about ½ cup peas, 1 lettuce wedge, and 2 tablespoons salad dressing per serving)

SERVE WITH

2 cups frozen green peas, steamed (10 ounces)

Calories 50; total fat 0g (saturated fat 0g); protein 4g; carbohydrates 10g; fiber 3g; cholesterol 0mg; sodium 80mg; vitamin A 30%; vitamin C 20%; calcium 2%; iron 6%

½ small head of iceberg lettuce, cut in 4 wedges and topped with ½ cup reduced-fat Thousand Island dressing or other reduced-fat dressing

Calories 80; total fat 4.5g (saturated fat 0.5g); protein 0g; carbohydrates 8g; fiber 0g; cholesterol 10mg; sodium 340mg; vitamin A 4%; vitamin C 2%; calcium 0%; iron 0%

Thyme-Rubbed Skillet Pork Chops

with Sweet Corn, Steamed Brussels Sprouts, and Wheat Rolls

Calories 350; total fat 9g (saturated fat 2.5g); protein 34g; carbohydrates 38g; fiber 8g; cholesterol 70mg; sodium 380mg; vitamin A 15%; vitamin C 150%; calcium 8%; iron 15%

½ **teaspoon dried thyme leaves**

¼ **teaspoon dried rosemary, crushed**

¼ **teaspoon garlic powder**

¼ **teaspoon paprika**

¼ **teaspoon salt**

¼ **teaspoon black pepper**

4 **pork chops with bone in (1¼ pounds total)**

1 **teaspoon canola oil**

▶ In a small bowl, combine the thyme, rosemary, garlic powder, paprika, salt, and pepper. Sprinkle evenly over both sides of the pork chops, pressing lightly to allow the thyme mixture to adhere.

▶ Place a large nonstick skillet over medium heat until hot, add the oil, and tilt the skillet to coat the bottom lightly. Add the pork chops and cook 5 minutes on each side or until barely pink in the center. Remove from heat, cover, and let stand 3 minutes to allow juices to release and create a light sauce.

Calories 170; total fat 7g (saturated fat 2g); protein 25g; carbohydrates 0g; fiber 0g; cholesterol 70mg; sodium 230mg; vitamin A 0%; vitamin C 2%; calcium 2%; iron 6%

TIME-SHAVER TIP: Allowing meat or poultry to rest (covered) a few minutes after the cooking is done is the "lazy" way to add interest, flavor, and a quick light au jus to the simplest cut on the busiest days.

Excellent source of fiber and vitamin C

Good source of vitamin A and iron

Makes 4 pork chops total

Serves 4 *(1 pork chop, about ½ cup corn, 1 cup brussels sprouts, and 1 roll per serving)*

SERVE WITH

2 cups frozen corn, boiled (10 ounces)

Calories 60; total fat 0.5g (saturated fat 0g); protein 2g; carbohydrates 15g; fiber 2g; cholesterol 0mg; sodium 0mg; vitamin A 4%; vitamin C 8%; calcium 0%; iron 2%

1 pound brussels sprouts, steamed (4 cups)

Calories 45; total fat 0g (saturated fat 0 g); protein 4g; carbohydrates 9g; fiber 4g; cholesterol 0mg; sodium 10mg; vitamin A 15%; vitamin C 140%; calcium 2%; iron 6%

4 1-ounce whole-wheat dinner rolls, warmed

Calories 80; total fat 1.5g (saturated fat 0g); protein 2g; carbohydrates 14g; fiber 2g; cholesterol 0mg; sodium 135mg; vitamin A 0%; vitamin C 0%; calcium 4%; iron 4%

Seared Pork Tenderloin and Horseradish-Rosemary Aioli

with Quick-Baked Potatoes, Lemon-Zested String Beans, and Caesar's Tomatoes

Calories 350; total fat 7g (saturated fat 1.5g); protein 30g; carbohydrates 42g; fiber 8g; cholesterol 80mg; sodium 460mg; vitamin A 25%; vitamin C 101%; calcium 10%; iron 20%

¼ teaspoon paprika, optional

¼ plus ⅛ teaspoon salt

⅛ teaspoon coarsely ground black pepper

1 pound pork tenderloin

¼ cup water

⅓ cup fat-free sour cream

1½ tablespoons light mayonnaise

2 teaspoons prepared horseradish

1 medium garlic clove, minced

¼ teaspoon dried rosemary, crushed

▶ Preheat the oven to 425°F.

▶ In a small bowl, combine the paprika, ¼ teaspoon salt, and pepper. Coat the pork evenly with the mixture. Place a medium skillet over medium-high heat until hot, and coat the skillet with cooking spray. Add the pork and cook 2 minutes, turn, and cook 2 minutes more or until browned. Place in an 11" × 7" baking pan coated with cooking spray.

▶ Add the water to the skillet, scraping the bottom and sides; bring to a boil and pour evenly over the pork. Bake 18 to 20 minutes or until the meat reaches an internal temperature of 150°F. Remove from the oven and let stand a few minutes in the baking pan on a cooling rack before removing and slicing.

▶ Meanwhile, in a small bowl, combine the remaining ingredients. Place the pork on a serving platter, drizzle with any accumulated juices, and serve with the sauce alongside.

Calories 180; total fat 6g (saturated fat 1.5g); protein 25g; carbohydrates 5g; fiber 0g; cholesterol 80mg; sodium 350mg; vitamin A 4%; vitamin C 6%; calcium 4%; iron 8%

COOK'S NOTE: *The pork will continue to cook while resting.*

Excellent source of fiber, vitamins A and C, and iron

Good source of calcium

Makes 12 ounces pork plus ½ cup sauce total

Serves 4 *(3 ounces pork, 2 tablespoons sauce, 1 potato, 1 tablespoon onion, 1 cup beans, and 3 to 4 tomato slices per serving)*

SERVE WITH

4 medium red potatoes (1½ pounds), pierced, microwaved on High for 11 minutes, and topped with ¼ cup chopped green onions

Calories 120; total fat 0g (saturated fat 0g); protein 3g; carbohydrates 28g; fiber 3g; cholesterol 0mg; sodium 45mg; vitamin A 0%; vitamin C 60%; calcium 2%; iron 6%

1 pound green beans, steamed and tossed with 2 tablespoons chopped parsley and 1 teaspoon grated lemon rind

Calories 25; total fat 0g (saturated fat 0g); protein 1g; carbohydrates 7g; fiber 4g; cholesterol 0mg; sodium 0mg; vitamin A 6%; vitamin C 15%; calcium 6%; iron 2%

3 medium tomatoes, sliced (3 cups), and 40 sprays of Caesar salad dressing spritzer

Calories 25; total fat 1g (saturated fat 0g); protein 1g; carbohydrates 4g; fiber 1g; cholesterol 0mg; sodium 70mg; vitamin A 15%; vitamin C 20%; calcium 0%; iron 2%

Spiced Pork and Dark Cherry–Ginger Salsa

with Quick-Baked Sweet Potato Halves and Lemon-Broccoli Florets

Calories 350; total fat 4.5g (saturated fat 1.5g); protein 29g; carbohydrates 51g; fiber 7g; cholesterol 75mg; sodium 260mg; vitamin A 480%; vitamin C 130%; calcium 8%; iron 15%

⅛ teaspoon ground allspice

¼ teaspoon salt

¼ teaspoon coarsely ground black pepper

1 pound pork tenderloin

½ 16-ounce package frozen dark sweet cherries, thawed and chopped coarse

1 small firm pear, peeled and diced (¾ cup)

⅓ cup dried cherries

¼ cup finely chopped red onion or 2 finely chopped jalapeño peppers

1 teaspoon grated gingerroot

▶ Preheat the oven to 425°F.

▶ In a small bowl, combine the allspice, salt, and pepper. Sprinkle evenly over the pork.

▶ Heat a medium nonstick skillet over medium-high heat until hot, and coat the skillet with cooking spray. Add the pork and cook 2 minutes, turn, and cook 2 minutes more to brown. Place in an 11″ × 7″ baking pan coated with cooking spray and bake 18 to 20 minutes or until the internal temperature reaches 150°F.

► Meanwhile, combine the sweet cherries, pear, dried cherries, onion, and ginger in a small bowl and stir until well blended. Set aside.

► Remove the pork from the oven and let stand a few minutes in the baking pan on a cooling rack before removing and slicing. Slice thin and serve with the cherry mixture.

Calories 240; total fat 4g (saturated fat 1.5g); protein 25g; carbohydrates 25g; fiber 2g; cholesterol 75mg; sodium 200mg; vitamin A 10%; vitamin C 6%; calcium 2%; iron 10%

COOK'S NOTE: *The pork will continue to cook while resting.*

TIME-SHAVER TIP: *Don't peel the pear.*

Excellent source of fiber and vitamins A and C

Good source of iron

Makes 12 ounces pork and about 2 cups cherry mixture total

Serves 4 *(3 ounces pork, ½ cup cherry mixture, ½ sweet potato, ¾ cup broccoli, and 1 lemon wedge per serving)*

SERVE WITH

2 medium sweet potatoes (12 ounces), pierced, cooked in the microwave on High for 10 minutes until tender, and halved

Calories 100; total fat 0g (saturated fat 0g); protein 2g; carbohydrates 23g; fiber 4g; cholesterol 0mg; sodium 40mg; vitamin A 440%; vitamin C 35%; calcium 4%; iron 4%

3 cups broccoli florets, steamed and served with 1 medium lemon, quartered

Calories 15; total fat 0g (saturated fat 0g); protein 2g; carbohydrates 3g; fiber 2g; cholesterol 0mg; sodium 15mg; vitamin A 30%; vitamin C 80%; calcium 2%; iron 2%

Pork Chops and Tarragon-Lemon Rice

with Asparagus Spear Salad and Toasted Sesame Seeds

Calories 350; total fat 9g (saturated fat 2.5g); protein 31g; carbohydrates 35g; fiber 4g; cholesterol 70mg; sodium 630mg; vitamin A 17%; vitamin C 10%; calcium 6%; iron 20%

¾ cup dry quick-cooking brown rice

¼ teaspoon dried tarragon leaves

¼ teaspoon garlic powder

½ teaspoon salt

¼ teaspoon black pepper

4 boneless pork chops, trimmed of fat (1 pound total)

1½ cups water

1 teaspoon grated lemon rind

1 tablespoon diet margarine

▶ Cook the rice with the tarragon in a small saucepan according to the package directions, omitting any salt or fat.

▶ Meanwhile, heat a medium nonstick skillet over medium heat until hot. In a small bowl, combine the garlic powder, ¼ teaspoon of the salt, and pepper. Sprinkle both sides of the pork with the garlic powder mixture. Coat the skillet with cooking spray; add the pork and cook 4 minutes on each side or until the meat is barely pink in the center. Remove from heat and place the pork on a separate plate.

▶ Add the cooked rice and remaining ingredients to the pan residue. Scrape the bottom of the skillet to release any drippings and mix it into the rice. Top with the pork.

Calories 300; total fat 8g (saturated fat 2g); protein 28g; carbohydrates 26g; fiber 2g; cholesterol 70mg; sodium 400mg; vitamin A 2%; vitamin C 2%; calcium 2%; iron 6%

COOK'S NOTE: *The pan residue provides a lot of great flavor, so be sure to stir well.*

Excellent source of iron
Good source of fiber and vitamins A and C

Makes 4 pork chops plus about 2½ cups rice mixture total

Serves 4 *(1 pork chop, scant ⅔ cup rice mixture, 4 to 5 spears asparagus, 1 tablespoon dressing, and ½ teaspoon sesame seeds per serving)*

SERVE WITH

1 pound asparagus (about 20 spears), cooked quickly, cooled under cold water, and topped with ¼ cup reduced-fat balsamic salad dressing and 2 teaspoons toasted sesame seeds

Calories 50; total fat 1g (saturated fat 0g); protein 3g; carbohydrates 9g; fiber 2g; cholesterol 0mg; sodium 240mg; vitamin A 15%; vitamin C 10%; calcium 4%; iron 15%

Speedy Chimichurri-Style Pork Chops

with Corn on the Cob and Fresh String Beans

Calories 350; total fat 10g (saturated fat 2.5g); protein 31g; carbohydrates 42g; fiber 6g; cholesterol 70mg; sodium 190mg; vitamin A 15%; vitamin C 30%; calcium 8%; iron 10%

3 tablespoons reduced-fat olive oil vinaigrette

¼ cup finely chopped fresh parsley

½ medium garlic clove, minced

1 teaspoon grated lemon rind

⅛ to ¼ teaspoon pepper flakes

4 boneless pork chops, trimmed of fat (1 pound total)

▶ Combine all the ingredients, except the pork, in a small bowl and stir until well blended. Place the pork chops on a plate and brush 1 tablespoon of the parsley mixture evenly over both sides of all. Let stand 15 minutes.

▶ Heat a large nonstick skillet over medium-high heat until hot, and coat the skillet with cooking spray. Add the pork chops and cook 4 minutes. Turn, reduce heat to medium, and cook 3 minutes or until barely pink in the center. Remove from heat, top with the remaining parsley mixture, and let stand 3 minutes to absorb flavors slightly.

Calories 190; total fat 8g (saturated fat 2.5g); protein 25g; carbohydrates 1g; fiber 0g; cholesterol 70mg; sodium 170mg; vitamin A 6%; vitamin C 10%; calcium 2%; iron 6%

COOK'S NOTE: To avoid cross-contamination, separate the tablespoon of the parsley mixture from the balance and place it in a separate bowl before brushing the raw meat.

Excellent source of fiber and vitamin C

Good source of vitamin A and iron

Makes 4 pork chops and ¼ cup parsley mixture total

Serves 4 *(1 pork chop, 1 tablespoon parsley mixture, 1 ear of corn, and 1 cup beans per serving)*

SERVE WITH

4 medium ears of corn, boiled

Calories 140; total fat 1.5g (saturated fat 0g); protein 5g; carbohydrates 34g; fiber 2g; cholesterol 0mg; sodium 20mg; vitamin A 2%; vitamin C 6%; calcium 0%; iron 0%

1 pound green beans, steamed (3½ cups)

Calories 25; total fat 0g (saturated fat 0g); protein 1g; carbohydrates 7g; fiber 4g; cholesterol 0mg; sodium 0mg; vitamin A 6%; vitamin C 15%; calcium 6%; iron 2%

Fresh Ginger–Pork Potsticker Bowls

with Spring Strawberry-Melon Salad and Sweet Vinaigrette

Calories 350; total fat 7g (saturated fat 2.5g); protein 17g; carbohydrates 57g; fiber 5g; cholesterol 30mg; sodium 1,340mg; vitamin A 50%; vitamin C 110%; calcium 10%; iron 20%

¼ pound ground pork

½ cup matchstick carrots, chopped fine

1 teaspoon grated gingerroot

⅛ teaspoon dried pepper flakes, optional

24 wonton wrappers

2 cups water

2 14.5-ounce cans reduced-sodium chicken broth

2 teaspoons light soy sauce

4 medium green onions, chopped fine (½ cup)

► Combine the pork, carrots, ginger, and pepper flakes in a small bowl and stir to blend thoroughly. Fill the wontons according to the package directions.

► Add the water to a Dutch oven; place a collapsible steamer basket inside. Arrange the wontons in a single layer on the steamer basket—do not stack the wontons on top of each other. Bring to a boil over medium-high heat. Cover and steam 13 minutes (add ½ cup additional water, if needed, after 8 minutes to keep the oven from boiling dry).

► Remove the basket (with the wontons in it) from the Dutch oven. Discard any remaining water. To the Dutch oven, add the broth; bring to a boil over high heat; then add the wontons. (Note: The wontons may stick together. Do not pull them apart; submerge the entire steamer basket containing the wontons in the broth, and they will release immediately.)

Return just to a boil, remove the Dutch oven from heat, and remove the wontons from the broth with a slotted spoon. Place six wontons in each of four shallow soup bowls. Add the soy sauce to the broth, and spoon ¾ cup of the broth over each serving of wontons. Sprinkle evenly with the green onion.

Calories 250; total fat 7g (saturated fat 2.5g); protein 15g; carbohydrates 30g; fiber 2g; cholesterol 30mg; sodium 880mg; vitamin A 20%; vitamin C 6%; calcium 6%; iron 15%

COOK'S NOTE: *It may take a few tries before you can successfully make the wrappers properly, but once you do, it comes quickly and is a valuable new technique.*

Excellent source of fiber, vitamins A and C, and iron

Good source of calcium

Makes about 4 cups broth and 24 wontons total

Serves 4 *(scant 1 cup broth, 6 wontons, 2 cups salad, and 2 tablespoons dressing per serving)*

SERVE WITH

4 cups baby spinach or spring greens topped with 2 cups sliced strawberries, 2 cups diced watermelon, ¼ cup chopped red onion, and ½ cup reduced-fat raspberry or ginger vinaigrette

Calories 110; total fat 0g (saturated fat 0g); protein 2g; carbohydrates 26g; fiber 3g; cholesterol 0mg; sodium 460mg; vitamin A 30%; vitamin C 100%; calcium 4%; iron 8%

Stuffed Quick-Baked Potatoes, Cheese Sauce, and Broccoli

with Vine-Ripened Tomato and Cucumber Salad

Calories 350; total fat 8g (saturated fat 4.5g); protein 16g; carbohydrates 55g; fiber 7g; cholesterol 20mg; sodium 970mg; vitamin A 50%; vitamin C 160%; calcium 30%; iron 15%

4 medium Yukon gold potatoes, scrubbed and pierced several times with a fork (1½ pounds total)

2 cups small broccoli florets (5 ounces)

¼ cup water

¾ cup fat-free milk

2 teaspoons cornstarch

1 tablespoon diet margarine

1 cup (4 ounces) reduced-fat shredded sharp cheddar cheese or 4 slices American cheese, torn into small pieces

1 to 2 teaspoons Worcestershire sauce

½ teaspoon salt

⅛ teaspoon cayenne

▶ Place the potatoes in the microwave and cook on High for 11 minutes or until tender when pierced with a fork. Set aside on a separate plate.

▶ Place the broccoli and water in a shallow microwave-safe pan or bowl, cover with plastic wrap, and microwave on High for 3 to 4 minutes or until tender crisp; drain well and set aside. Cover to keep warm.

▶ Meanwhile, bring all but 2 tablespoons of the milk to a simmer over medium heat in a medium saucepan. Combine the remaining 2 tablespoons milk with the cornstarch, and stir until cornstarch is completely dissolved. Whisk into the milk in the saucepan and continue to simmer slightly

2 minutes, stirring frequently. Remove from heat and whisk in the margarine until melted. Whisk in the cheese, Worcestershire sauce, salt, and cayenne until the cheese is melted.

▶ To assemble, cut the potatoes almost in half lengthwise, fluff with a fork, spoon equal amounts of the cheese sauce over each potato, and top with broccoli.

Calories 300; total fat 8g (saturated fat 4.5g); protein 14g; carbohydrates 43g; fiber 5g; cholesterol 20mg; sodium 620mg; vitamin A 30%; vitamin C 130%; calcium 30%; iron 10%

COOK'S NOTE: Yukon gold potatoes are often sold in 5-pound bags. Russet potatoes may be used, if preferred, but their texture will be a bit drier than that of the Yukon gold potatoes.

Excellent source of fiber, vitamins A and C, and calcium

Good source of iron

Makes 4 stuffed potatoes plus 1 cup sauce total

Serves 4 *(1 potato, ½ cup broccoli, ¼ cup sauce, plus about 1⅓ cups sliced tomatoes and cucumber and 1½ tablespoons dressing per serving)*

SERVE WITH

4 medium tomatoes, sliced (4 cups), and ½ medium cucumber, peeled and sliced (1 cup), topped with 6 tablespoons fat-free salad dressing

Calories 50; total fat 0g (saturated fat 0g); protein 1g; carbohydrates 12g; fiber 2g; cholesterol 0mg; sodium 350mg; vitamin A 20%; vitamin C 30%; calcium 2%; iron 2%

Feta, Edamame, and Fresh Herb Penne

with Tender Baby Spinach, Red Onion, and Grapefruit Salad with Raspberry Vinaigrette

Calories 340; total fat 9g (saturated fat 2g); protein 15g; carbohydrates 51g; fiber 8g; cholesterol 5mg; sodium 650mg; vitamin A 40%; vitamin C 50%; calcium 10%; iron 15%

6 ounces uncooked multigrain penne or rotini

1 cup (5 ounces) frozen shelled edamame, thawed

1 cup (5 ounces) sweet grape tomatoes, quartered

1 tablespoon fresh oregano leaves

¾ teaspoon fresh rosemary leaves, chopped

2 medium garlic cloves, minced

1 tablespoon extra-virgin olive oil

½ teaspoon salt

¾ cup (3 ounces) crumbled reduced-fat feta cheese

▶ Cook the pasta according to the package directions, omitting any salt or fat. Add the edamame during the last 5 minutes of cooking time. Drain the pasta mixture, reserving ¼ cup of the liquid. Combine the pasta mixture and its liquid with all remaining ingredients, except the feta, in a pasta or medium bowl. Sprinkle with the feta and toss gently. Serve hot or at room temperature.

Calories 290; total fat 8g (saturated fat 2g); protein 14g; carbohydrates 39g; fiber 6g; cholesterol 5mg; sodium 590mg; vitamin A 15%; vitamin C 15%; calcium 8%; iron 10%

Makes 5 cups pasta mixture total

Serves 4 *(1¼ cups pasta mixture, 1¾ cups salad, and 1 tablespoon vinaigrette per serving)*

SERVE WITH

4 cups baby spinach, ½ medium red onion, sliced (½ cup), and 1 cup grapefruit sections topped with ¼ cup fat-free raspberry vinaigrette

Calories 50; total fat 0g (saturated fat 0g); protein 1g; carbohydrates 12g; fiber 2g; cholesterol 0mg; sodium 55mg; vitamin A 30%; vitamin C 40%; calcium 2%; iron 4%

🥄 **COOK'S NOTE:** *Be sure to use fresh herbs in this dish to make it pop with flavor. Edamame are soybeans, which are sold in major supermarkets and health food stores. They can be purchased in the pod or shelled.*

Excellent source of fiber and vitamins A and C

Good source of calcium and iron

Skillet Rice and Black Beans

with Shredded Lettuce, Avocado, and Tomato Salad and Warmed Soft Corn Tortillas

Calories 350; total fat 11g (saturated fat 1.5g); protein 10g; carbohydrates 53g; fiber 12g; cholesterol 5mg; sodium 545mg; vitamin A 45%; vitamin C 45%; calcium 15%; iron 15%

1 large yellow onion, chopped (1½ cups)

1½ cups water

¾ cup quick-cooking brown rice

1 15-ounce can black beans, rinsed and drained

1 4-ounce can chopped mild green chilies

½ 1.25-ounce packet chili seasoning

2 teaspoons extra-virgin olive oil

½ cup fat-free sour cream

2 to 3 tablespoons chopped fresh cilantro leaves

▶ Heat a large nonstick skillet over medium-high heat until hot, and coat the skillet with cooking spray. Add the onion, coat with cooking spray, and cook 6 minutes or until the edges begin to brown, stirring frequently.

▶ Stir in the water, rice, beans, and chilies. Bring to a boil over medium-high heat. Reduce heat, cover, and simmer 14 minutes or until the water is absorbed. Remove from heat, and add the chili seasoning and oil. Let stand 5 minutes, covered. Serve topped with the sour cream and cilantro.

Calories 210; total fat 4g (saturated fat 0.5g); protein 7g; carbohydrates 35g; fiber 6g; cholesterol 5mg; sodium 530mg; vitamin A 6%; vitamin C 15%; calcium 10%; iron 10%

COOK'S NOTE: *For a moister consistency, add ½ cup water after the 5-minute standing time.*

Excellent source of fiber and vitamins A and C

Good source of calcium and iron

Makes about 6 cups rice-and-bean mixture total

Serves 4 *(1½ cups rice-and-bean mixture, ½ cup lettuce, ¼ cup avocado, 2 tablespoons tomato, and 1 tortilla per serving)*

SERVE WITH

Top the rice-and-bean mixture with 2 cups shredded lettuce; 1 medium avocado, seeded and chopped (1 cup); ½ medium tomato, chopped (½ cup); and the juice of 1 medium lime

Calories 80; total fat 7g (saturated fat 1g); protein 1g; carbohydrates 6g; fiber 4g; cholesterol 0mg; sodium 5mg; vitamin A 40%; vitamin C 25%; calcium 2%; iron 4%

4 soft corn tortillas, warmed

Calories 60; total fat 0.5g (saturated fat 0g); protein 1g; carbohydrates 12g; fiber 2g; cholesterol 0mg; sodium 10mg; vitamin A 0%; vitamin C 0%; calcium 2%; iron 2%

Skillet Garden au Gratin

with Baby Limas and Creamy Dill Cucumbers

Calories 350; total fat 8g (saturated fat 4g); protein 16g; carbohydrates 54g; fiber 9g; cholesterol 20mg; sodium 1,160mg; vitamin A 15%; vitamin C 70%; calcium 25%; iron 15%

1 medium yellow onion, chopped (1 cup)

1 medium yellow squash, sliced thin (1 cup)

1 medium zucchini, sliced thin (1 cup)

1 cup (5 ounces) frozen corn, thawed

1 10.75-ounce can reduced-fat cream of mushroom condensed soup

¼ cup water

¼ teaspoon dried thyme or sage

⅛ teaspoon salt

¾ cup (3 ounces) shredded reduced-fat sharp cheddar cheese

½ cup cornbread stuffing

▶ Preheat the oven to 350°F.

▶ Heat a medium nonstick skillet over medium heat until hot, and coat the skillet with cooking spray. Add the onion, coat with cooking spray, and cook 4 minutes or until the onion is translucent, stirring frequently. Add the yellow squash, zucchini, corn, ½ the soup, water, and thyme. Stir until well blended, and bring to a boil over medium-high heat; cover and cook (still over medium-high heat) 3 minutes or until squash is tender, stirring after 2 minutes.

▶ Remove from heat; stir in the salt. Top with the remaining soup, using the back of a spoon to spread evenly over all. Sprinkle evenly with the cheese and cornbread stuffing. Bake, uncovered, 10 minutes or until bubbly around the edges. Remove from the oven and let stand 5 minutes to absorb flavors.

Calories 210; total fat 7g (saturated fat 4g); protein 10g; carbohydrates 27g; fiber 4g; cholesterol 20mg; sodium 900mg; vitamin A 8%; vitamin C 40%; calcium 20%; iron 6%

COOK'S NOTE: *For a variation, try adding 2 cups coarsely chopped (not shredded) cabbage while cooking the onion, for more volume without added calories or fat.*

Excellent source of fiber, vitamin C, and calcium

Good source of vitamin A and iron

Makes 1 9-inch casserole total

Serves 4 *(¼ casserole, ½ cup lima beans, ¾ cup cucumber slices, and 1 tablespoon dressing per serving)*

SERVE WITH

2 cups frozen baby limas, steamed (10 ounces)

Calories 100; total fat 0g (saturated fat 0g); protein 5g; carbohydrates 18g; fiber 4g; cholesterol 0mg; sodium 85mg; vitamin A 4%; vitamin C 25%; calcium 2%; iron 8%

1½ medium cucumbers, peeled, sliced (3 cups), drizzled with ¼ cup fat-free ranch dressing, and sprinkled with ¼ teaspoon dried dill weed

Calories 40; total fat 0g (saturated fat 0g); protein 1g; carbohydrates 9g; fiber 1g; cholesterol 0mg; sodium 180mg; vitamin A 4%; vitamin C 10%; calcium 2%; iron 2%

Pinto Bean Shepherd's Pie

with Summer Squash Stir-Fry and Spinach-Mandarin Salad

Calories 340; total fat 8g (saturated fat 4g); protein 17g; carbohydrates 53g; fiber 10g; cholesterol 20mg; sodium 1,140mg; vitamin A 60%; vitamin C 160%; calcium 25%; iron 20%

½ 22-ounce package frozen mashed potatoes

1⅓ cups fat-free milk

¼ teaspoon salt

1 medium onion, chopped fine (1 cup)

½ 8-ounce package sliced mushrooms, chopped coarse

⅓ cup water

1 15-ounce can pinto beans, rinsed and drained

⅓ cup medium picante sauce

½ to ¾ teaspoon ground cumin

¾ cup (3 ounces) shredded reduced-fat sharp cheddar cheese

▶ Prepare the potatoes according to the package directions with the 1⅓ cups milk and ¼ teaspoon salt.

▶ Meanwhile, place a medium nonstick skillet over medium-high heat until hot, and coat the skillet with cooking spray. Add the onion, coat with cooking spray, and cook 6 minutes or until beginning to turn a rich brown. Add the mushrooms and cook 3 minutes. Stir in the water, beans, picante sauce, and cumin; cook 1 minute or until thoroughly heated. Using a fork or potato masher, mash the bean mixture. Remove from heat.

▶ Spoon the potatoes evenly over all, sprinkle with the cheese, cover with foil, and let stand 5 minutes to absorb flavors.

Calories 270; total fat 8g (saturated fat 3.5g); protein 13g; carbohydrates 36g; fiber 6g; cholesterol 20mg; sodium 660mg; vitamin A 8%; vitamin C 15%; calcium 20%; iron 6%

TIME-SHAVER TIP: *Be sure to buy sliced mushrooms and then chop them yourself. The sliced variety is cleaned before packaging, whereas the whole mushrooms are not. This will definitely save time..*

Excellent source of fiber, vitamins A and C, calcium, and iron

Makes about 5 cups bean-and-potato mixture total

Serves 4 *(about 1¼ cups bean-and-potato mixture, ½ cup squash, 2 tablespoons bell pepper, about 1¾ cups salad, 2 tablespoons dressing, and ¼ cup oranges per serving)*

SERVE WITH

2 medium zucchini or yellow squash, quartered lengthwise and cut into 1-inch pieces (2 cups), with ½ medium red bell pepper, sliced (½ cup), stir-fried in cooking spray

Calories 25; total fat 0g (saturated fat 0g); protein 3g; carbohydrates 4g; fiber 1g; cholesterol 0mg; sodium 0mg; vitamin A 15%; vitamin C 110%; calcium 2%; iron 4%

6 cups packed baby spinach and ¼ cup sliced onion tossed with ½ cup fat-free red wine vinegar salad dressing and topped with 1 cup mandarin oranges

Calories 50; total fat 0g (saturated fat 0g); protein 1g; carbohydrates 13g; fiber 3g; cholesterol 0mg; sodium 480mg; vitamin A 40%; vitamin C 40%; calcium 4%; iron 8%

5

Desserts

FROZEN DESSERTS

▶ Open-Face Frozen S'mores

▶ Raspberry Cream Goblets

▶ Cheater's Gelato

▶ Dark Cherry–Espresso Soft-Serve Ice Cream

▶ Apricot-Mango Creamy Coolers

▶ Orange Freezers

▶ Chocolate-Mocha Ice-Cream Sodas

NO-BAKE PIES

▶ Frozen Banana–Peanut Butter Pie

▶ Fresh Berry Cream Tarts

▶ No-Cook Pumpkin Custard Tarts

▶ No-Waiting Pineapple-Banana Pudding "Pie"

COOKIES

▶ New-Fashioned, Old-Fashioned Oatmeal Cookies

▶ Peppermint Brownie Splatter Cookies

▶ Pudding Snack Graham Cookies

▶ Cranberry–Chocolate Chip Chewies

CAKES AND MORE

▶ Angel Cake with Fresh Limed Fruit

▶ Featherlight Chocolate-Raspberry Almond Cupcakes

▶ Double-Fruit, Double-Citrus Cake Squares

▶ Banana Snack Squares with Pineapple and Coconut

▶ Gingerbread Rounds with Lemon Topping

▶ Chocolate Chip and Banana Pudding Cakes

▶ Blackberry Shortcakers

▶ Apricot Wheels

FRUIT-BASED DESSERTS

▶ Lemon-Orange Cream Bowls

▶ Tropical Fruit Custard Cups

▶ Fresh Fruit in Rich Cinnamon Cream

▶ Watermelon-Cranberry Splash

▶ Chai-Poached Pears and Blueberries

▶ Hot Butterscotch Apples and Ice Cream

▶ Sour Cherry–Almond Pear Parfaits

Open-Face Frozen S'mores

Calories 150; total fat 4g (saturated fat 1.5g); protein 2g; carbohydrates 30g; fiber 2g; cholesterol 0mg; sodium 110mg; vitamin A 0%; vitamin C 0%; calcium 2%; iron 4%

8 graham cracker squares, 2½-inch squares each

64 mini marshmallows (about ¾ cup total)

2 tablespoons plus 2 teaspoons mini semisweet chocolate chips

½ cup 98% fat-free chocolate ice cream

> **Makes 8 s'mores total**
>
> **Serves 4** (2 s'mores per serving)

▶ Preheat the broiler.

▶ Arrange the graham crackers on a foil-lined cookie sheet. Top each graham cracker with eight marshmallows and 1 teaspoon chocolate chips. Broil at least 4 inches away from heat source, 1½ minutes or until just beginning to brown.

▶ Remove from heat. Top each s'more with 1 tablespoon ice cream. Serve immediately or place in the freezer until needed.

COOK'S NOTE: Watch the s'mores closely while broiling to be sure the edges of the crackers do not burn.

Raspberry Cream Goblets

Calories 150; total fat 0g (saturated fat 0g); protein 3g; carbohydrates 32g; fiber 4g; cholesterol 0mg; sodium 65mg; vitamin A 10%; vitamin C 15%; calcium 10%; iron 0%

2 tablespoons plus 2 teaspoons amaretto, raspberry liqueur, or pomegranate juice

1⅔ cups fresh raspberries

2 teaspoons pourable sugar substitute, such as Splenda

2 cups fat-free vanilla ice cream

Makes 2 cups ice cream and about 1⅓ cups berry mixture total

Serves 4 (*½ cup ice cream and rounded ⅓ cup berry mixture per serving*)

▶ Combine all the ingredients, except the ice cream, in a medium bowl and toss gently yet thoroughly to blend.

▶ Spoon equal amounts of the ice cream into each of four wine goblets or dessert bowls, and spoon equal amounts of the berry mixture over the ice cream.

COOK'S NOTE: *You don't have to buy a large bottle of amaretto. Many stores sell the miniatures.*

Good source of fiber, vitamins A and C, and calcium

Cheater's Gelato

Calories 150; total fat 0.5g (saturated fat 0g); protein 2g; carbohydrates 36g; fiber 5g; cholesterol 0mg; sodium 10mg; vitamin A 8%; vitamin C 420%; calcium 4%; iron 6%

5 cups frozen whole strawberries

1 cup frozen peach slices, partially thawed

¾ cup pomegranate juice

¼ cup pourable sugar substitute, such as Splenda

1 teaspoon vanilla extract

Makes 4 cups gelato total

Serves 4 *(1 cup gelato per serving)*

▶ Combine all ingredients, except 2 cups of the strawberries, in a blender and puree until smooth. Add the remaining strawberries and again puree until smooth. (For a thinner consistency, add ¼ cup water.) Spoon equal amounts into four wine goblets or dessert bowls.

▶ Freeze leftovers in an airtight container. If the gelato is frozen solid, let it stand on the counter for 15 to 20 minutes to soften slightly.

COOK'S NOTE: *Pomegranate juice is sold in a variety of flavors and can be found in the produce section of your supermarket.*

Excellent source of fiber and vitamin C

Dark Cherry–Espresso Soft-Serve Ice Cream

Calories 150; total fat 1.5g (saturated fat 1g); protein 4g; carbohydrates 36g; fiber 4g; cholesterol 5mg; sodium 55mg; vitamin A 6%; vitamin C 2%; calcium 10%; iron 4%

2 cups 98% fat-free chocolate or vanilla ice cream

2 teaspoons instant coffee granules

½ 1-pound package frozen unsweetened dark cherries, partially thawed and halved

1 tablespoon chocolate syrup, such as Hershey's

> Makes 2 cups ice cream total
>
> Serves 4 (½ *cup ice cream per serving*)

▶ Place the ice cream in a medium bowl, sprinkle the coffee granules evenly over it, and combine gently yet thoroughly. (The granules may not be totally dissolved at this point.) Fold in the cherries.

▶ Spoon equal amounts into each of four wine glasses or dessert bowls, and drizzle chocolate syrup evenly over all. Or cover and place in the freezer until needed; drizzle chocolate over ice cream at time of serving.

COOK'S NOTE: *If the ice cream is too hard to work with, let stand on counter about 15 to 20 minutes to soften slightly before adding the other ingredients.*

Good source of fiber and calcium

Apricot-Mango Creamy Coolers

Calories 150; total fat 0g (saturated fat 0g); protein 3g; carbohydrates 35g; fiber 2g; cholesterol 0mg; sodium 75mg; vitamin A 30%; vitamin C 80%; calcium 8%; iron 2%

Makes 4 cups cooler total

Serves 4 *(1 cup cooler per serving)*

2 cups fresh or frozen diced mango

⅔ cup apricot nectar

1½ cups fat-free vanilla ice cream

1 12-ounce can diet lemon-lime soda or diet ginger ale

► Combine all ingredients, except 1 cup of the diet soda, in a blender. Blend until smooth; stir in the remaining diet soda and pour into four tall glasses.

COOK'S NOTE: *Be sure to stir in the 1 cup soda after the other ingredients have been pureed in the blender.*

Excellent source of vitamins A and C

Orange Freezers

Calories 150; total fat 1.5g (saturated fat 1g); protein 2g; carbohydrates 33g; fiber 4g; cholesterol 0mg; sodium 55mg; vitamin A 80%; vitamin C 90%; calcium 6%; iron 2%

3 cups fresh, or frozen and partially thawed, cantaloupe cubes

¼ cup lemon juice

2 cups orange sherbet

Makes 4 cups smoothie total

Serves 4 (*1 cup smoothie per serving*)

▶ Combine the cantaloupe and lemon juice in a blender and puree until smooth. Add the sherbet and again puree until smooth. Pour into four glasses and serve immediately.

COOK'S NOTE: *Store leftovers in an airtight container in the freezer. When ready to use, let stand 15 to 20 minutes to soften slightly, stir, and serve.*

TIME-SHAVER TIP: *If you're using a fresh cantaloupe, store the leftovers in an airtight container and freeze for a later use, such as another smoothie. This is a great way to stock up on frozen fruits to keep on hand without wasting any!*

Excellent source of vitamins A and C

Good source of fiber

Chocolate-Mocha Ice-Cream Sodas

Calories 150; total fat 0g (saturated fat 0g); protein 3g; carbohydrates 35g; fiber 1g; cholesterol 0mg; sodium 80mg; vitamin A 10%; vitamin C 0%; calcium 10%; iron 0%

Makes 4 sodas total

Serves 4 (1 cup ice-cream soda per serving)

1½ tablespoons instant coffee granules

2 tablespoons water

3 tablespoons chocolate syrup, such as Hershey's

2 cups fat-free vanilla or chocolate ice cream

1⅓ cups club soda

½ cup fat-free whipped topping

4 maraschino cherries, optional

▶ Combine the coffee granules and water in a small bowl, and stir until the coffee is completely dissolved. Stir in the syrup until well blended.

▶ Spoon ½ cup ice cream into each of four tall glasses; pour equal amounts of the chocolate syrup mixture, then the club soda, over each. Top each soda with whipped topping and a cherry, if desired.

COOK'S NOTE: The addition of coffee doesn't provide a coffee flavor; instead, it brings out the deep flavors of the chocolate without adding more fat and calories!

Good source of vitamin A and calcium

Frozen Banana–Peanut Butter Pie

Calories 150; total fat 3g (saturated fat 0.5g); protein 4g; carbohydrates 28g; fiber 2g; cholesterol 0mg; sodium 120mg; vitamin A 8%; vitamin C 4%; calcium 8%; iron 2%

3½ cups fat-free vanilla ice cream

3 tablespoons reduced-fat peanut butter

1 prepared graham cracker crust

2 small ripe bananas, peeled and sliced

Ground nutmeg to taste

Makes 1 8-inch pie total

Serves 8 (*1 wedge per serving*)

▶ Combine ½ cup of the ice cream with the peanut butter in a small bowl, stir until well blended, and set aside.

▶ Working quickly, spoon the remaining 3 cups ice cream into the bottom of the graham cracker crust. Using a teaspoon, spoon the peanut butter mixture evenly over the top. Arrange the banana slices over the peanut butter mixture and sprinkle lightly with the nutmeg. Serve immediately for a soft-serve ice cream, or cover and freeze until firm.

COOK'S NOTE: *If the pie is too hard to cut after it is frozen, allow it to stand at room temperature for 15 to 20 minutes to soften slightly for easier slicing.*

Fresh Berry Cream Tarts

Calories 150; total fat 6g (saturated fat 1g); protein 2g; carbohydrates 24g; fiber 1g; cholesterol 0mg; sodium 140mg; vitamin A 4%; vitamin C 50%; calcium 6%; iron 4%

Makes 6 tarts total

Serves 6 (*1 tart per serving*)

2 tablespoons apricot fruit spread

6 mini graham cracker piecrusts

1 6-ounce container nonfat lemon or vanilla yogurt sweetened with aspartame

2 cups quartered strawberries

▶ Place fruit spread in a small microwave-safe bowl and cook on High for 10 seconds to melt slightly. Spoon 1 teaspoon into each of the tart shells. Top each tart with 2 tablespoons yogurt and ⅓ cup berries.

COOK'S NOTE: *This is also good with strawberry fruit spread in place of the apricot.*

Excellent source of vitamin C

No-Cook Pumpkin Custard Tarts

Calories 150; total fat 7g (saturated fat 2g); protein 3g; carbohydrates 20g; fiber 1g; cholesterol 5mg; sodium 290mg; vitamin A 120%; vitamin C 2%; calcium 8%; iron 6%

½ 15-ounce can solid pumpkin

½ 1-ounce package instant sugar-free, fat-free banana cream or vanilla pudding mix

1 cup light vanilla soy milk or fat-free milk

2 tablespoons light cream cheese, tub style

¾ teaspoon ground cinnamon

6 mini graham cracker piecrusts

Makes 6 tarts total
Serves 6 *(1 tart per serving)*

▶ Combine all ingredients, except the tart shells, in a blender and puree until smooth. Spoon about ⅓ cup of the pumpkin mixture into each tart shell.

▶ Serve immediately, or refrigerate until needed.

COOK'S NOTE: *For peak texture, serve the tarts the same day they are filled. Otherwise, do not fill until serving time. The shells will become a bit soft if filled too far in advance.*

Excellent source of vitamin A

No-Waiting Pineapple-Banana Pudding "Pie"

Calories 150; total fat 1g (saturated fat 0g); protein 3g; carbohydrates 32g; fiber 2g; cholesterol 0mg; sodium 230mg; vitamin A 2%; vitamin C 10%; calcium 4%; iron 4%

Makes 6 cups "pie" total

Serves 8 (¾ cup "pie" per serving)

1 cup fat-free milk

1 1-ounce package instant sugar-free, fat-free banana cream or vanilla pudding mix

1 8-ounce container frozen fat-free whipped topping, thawed

2 ripe medium bananas, peeled and sliced (about 1½ cups)

7 graham cracker squares, 2½-inch squares each, crushed

¼ cup wheat germ

⅛ teaspoon ground nutmeg

1 8-ounce can pineapple tidbits or crushed pineapple in juice, drained

▶ Combine the milk and pudding mix in a large bowl and whisk until smooth. Stir in the whipped topping.

▶ Place ½ the banana slices evenly in the bottom of an 11″ × 7″ baking dish, spoon ½ the pudding mixture evenly over the bananas, and top with ½ the cracker crumbs. Sprinkle 2 tablespoons of the wheat germ and all of the nutmeg evenly over all. Repeat layers. Spread the pineapple evenly over all.

TIME-SHAVER TIP: *To crush graham crackers quickly without making a mess, simply place them in a small plastic bag, seal, and press down with the palm of your hand—or use the bottom of a bottle and tap lightly until crushed. Then discard the bag.*

Good source of vitamin C

New-Fashioned, Old-Fashioned Oatmeal Cookies

Calories 150; total fat 4.5g (saturated fat 0g); protein 2g; carbohydrates 26g; fiber 1g; cholesterol 20mg; sodium 135mg; vitamin A 0%; vitamin C 0%; calcium 2%; iron 6%

Makes 24 cookies total

Serves 12 *(2 cookies per serving)*

3 tablespoons canola oil

1 large egg

1¼ cups old-fashioned-style rolled oats

⅓ cup all-purpose flour

⅓ cup granulated sugar

¼ cup packed light brown sugar

¾ teaspoon baking soda

¼ teaspoon salt

1 cup raisins

▶ Preheat the oven to 375°F.

▶ Combine the oil and egg in a medium bowl. Using an electric mixer on high speed, beat until well blended. Add the remaining ingredients, except the raisins, and reduce to medium speed; beat until well blended. Stir in the raisins.

▶ Lightly coat two nonstick cookie sheets with cooking spray. Using a tablespoon measure, spoon six cookies onto each cookie sheet. (Do not put more than six on a sheet, because they will spread while baking.) Bake 6 minutes or until slightly golden on the edges and light in the middle. They will not look done at this point but will continue to cook while cooling. Remove from the oven and let stand on the cookie sheet 3 minutes before removing. Continue with remaining batter.

TIME-SHAVER TIP: Short on cookie sheets and need to cool a hot one down fast? Pop it into your freezer for a couple of minutes.

Peppermint Brownie Splatter Cookies

Calories 150; total fat 5g (saturated fat 1.5g); protein 2g; carbohydrates 26g; fiber 1g; cholesterol 30mg; sodium 90mg; vitamin A 0%; vitamin C 0%; calcium 0%; iron 6%

2 large eggs

1 tablespoon plus 1 teaspoon canola oil

2 teaspoons instant coffee granules

1 10.5-ounce package fudge brownie mix

12 small peppermint patties, such as York, cut into ⅛-inch pieces

1 tablespoon powdered sugar

▶ Preheat the oven to 350°F.

▶ In a medium bowl, combine the eggs, oil, and coffee granules. Stir until well blended; the coffee granules may not be totally dissolved at this point. Stir in the brownie mix until just blended; the batter will be very stiff. Gently but thoroughly stir the candies into the batter.

▶ Liberally coat two large nonstick cookie sheets with cooking spray, or line them with parchment paper. Using a tablespoon measure, spoon 6 scant tablespoons of the batter onto the cookie sheet, leaving about 4 inches between the cookies. Bake 5 minutes or until faint surface bubbles appear (as when cooking pancakes). Cookies will not appear done at this point. Place the cookie sheet on a cooling rack 1 full minute. Coat a flat spatula with cooking spray and gently remove the cookies, placing them directly on the cooling rack to cool completely.

▶ Repeat, alternating the cookie sheets to start with a cool sheet each time.

▶ When the cookies are cool, dust powdered sugar evenly over them using a fine sieve. Store them in an airtight container with a sheet of waxed paper between layers to prevent cookies from sticking together.

COOK'S NOTE: *Kids of all ages love these cookies; they're fun to make, fun to look at, and even more fun to eat.*

TIME-SHAVER TIP: *Parchment paper is sold alongside foil and plastic wrap in your supermarket. Use it for extra-easy baking.*

Pudding Snack Graham Cookies

Calories 150; total fat 3.5g (saturated fat 0.5g); protein 3g; carbohydrates 26g; fiber 1g; cholesterol 0mg; sodium 200mg; vitamin A 0%; vitamin C 0%; calcium 4%; iron 6%

Makes 8 cookies total

Serves 4 *(2 cookies per serving)*

2 4-ounce containers sugar-free, fat-free chocolate pudding snack packs

¼ cup fat-free whipped topping

4 teaspoons reduced-fat creamy or crunchy peanut butter

8 graham cracker squares, 2½-inch squares each

▶ Combine the pudding and whipped topping in a small bowl and stir until well blended.

▶ Spread ½ teaspoon peanut butter on each graham cracker square, and top with equal amounts of the pudding mixture. Serve immediately, or freeze 1 hour.

COOK'S NOTE: *After the cookies are frozen, you may wrap them individually to keep on hand for a quick frozen treat.*

Cranberry–Chocolate Chip Chewies

Calories 150; total fat 6g (saturated fat 1.5g); protein 3g; carbohydrates 24g; fiber 2g; cholesterol 0mg; sodium 15mg; vitamin A 6%; vitamin C 0%; calcium 2%; iron 4%

16 foil or paper candy liners

¾ cup plus 2 tablespoons mini marshmallows

¼ cup dried cranberries

3 tablespoons mini semisweet chocolate chips

¼ cup (1 ounce) sliced almonds, toasted and crumbled coarse

> **Makes 16 chewies total**
>
> **Serves 4** (4 chewies per serving)

▶ Preheat the oven to 325°F.

▶ Place the liners in an 8-inch square baking pan or two mini muffin pans. Coat the liners with cooking spray. Fill each liner with about five or six marshmallows. Sprinkle evenly with the cranberries, chocolate chips, and nuts.

▶ Bake 5 minutes or until the marshmallows are no longer puffy. Remove from the oven and place on a cooling rack (in the pan) to cool completely. When cool, store in an airtight container in the pantry.

COOK'S NOTE: These are even better the next day—and the next.

Angel Cake with Fresh Limed Fruit

Calories 150; total fat 0.5g (saturated fat 0g); protein 3g; carbohydrates 35g; fiber 4g; cholesterol 0mg; sodium 220mg; vitamin A 15%; vitamin C 180%; calcium 8%; iron 4%

Makes 24 cake slices total

Serves 12 (2 cake slices and about ¾ cup fruit per serving)

6 medium limes

1 tablespoon grated fresh gingerroot

¼ cup pourable sugar substitute, such as Splenda

1 9-inch angel food cake

6 cups sliced strawberries

6 ripe kiwifruit, peeled and chopped (3 cups)

3 15-ounce cans mandarin oranges, drained

▶ Grate 1 tablespoon lime rind and place in a small bowl. Squeeze the juice from all of the limes; add to the rind with the ginger and sugar substitute. Stir until well blended.

▶ Using a serrated knife, slice the cake into 24 pieces. To serve, place two cake slices on each dessert plate, top with ½ cup strawberries, ¼ cup kiwifruit, and ¼ cup oranges. Spoon 1 tablespoon of the lime mixture evenly over the fruit. Let stand 5 minutes, if desired, to allow the cake to absorb some of the liquid.

TIME-SHAVER TIP: If serving a large crowd, place the cake slices in a fanned-out fashion on a large platter. Toss the strawberries with the lime mixture, and spoon this evenly over the cake slices; top with the oranges and kiwi. Let stand a few minutes to let the cake absorb the liquid slightly.

Excellent source of vitamin C

Good source of fiber and vitamin A

Featherlight Chocolate-Raspberry Almond Cupcakes

Calories 150; total fat 6g (saturated fat 1g); protein 2g; carbohydrates 22g; fiber 1g; cholesterol 0mg; sodium 150mg; vitamin A 0%; vitamin C 0%; calcium 2%; iron 4%

Makes 24 cupcakes total

Serves 24 (*1 cupcake per serving*)

1 18.25-ounce package devil's food cake mix

1 12-ounce can diet cola, such as Dr. Pepper

½ cup egg substitute

2 tablespoons canola oil

½ cup raspberry fruit spread

1 cup (4 ounces) sliced almonds, toasted

▶ Preheat the oven to 325°F. Lightly coat two 12-cup nonstick muffin tins with cooking spray and set aside.

▶ Combine the cake mix, cola, egg substitute, and oil in a medium bowl and mix according to the package directions. Spoon equal amounts into each muffin cup, and bake 15 minutes or until a wooden pick inserted in the center comes out clean.

▶ Place the fruit spread in a small microwave-safe bowl and cook on High for 30 seconds or until slightly melted. Stir and spoon 1 teaspoon of the fruit spread onto each cupcake, using the back of the spoon to spread quickly. Sprinkle the almonds evenly over all. Serve immediately, or cool completely before storing leftovers in an airtight container in the pantry.

COOK'S NOTE: *Buy one bottle of cola from a soda machine instead of a larger amount, if desired.*

Double-Fruit, Double-Citrus Cake Squares

Calories 150; total fat 4g (saturated fat 1g); protein 2g; carbohydrates 27g; fiber 2g; cholesterol 0mg; sodium 180mg; vitamin A 4%; vitamin C 45%; calcium 2%; iron 4%

Makes 1 15″ × 10″ cake plus about 6½ cups fruit total

Serves 20 (1 2½″ × 3″ cake square and about ⅓ cup fruit mixture per serving)

1 18.25-ounce package yellow cake mix

¾ cup egg substitute

½ cup water

Grated rind and juice of 2 medium lemons

Grated rind and juice of 1 medium orange

2 tablespoons canola oil

4 cups sliced strawberries

2 ripe mangoes, peeled, seeded, and chopped (about 2 cups)

3 tablespoons pourable sugar substitute, such as Splenda

▶ Preheat the oven to 350°F. Coat a 15″ × 10″ jelly-roll pan with cooking spray and set aside.

▶ Combine the cake mix, egg substitute, water, lemon rind and juice, orange rind and juice, and oil in a medium bowl. Mix according to the package directions. Pour the batter into the pan and bake 13 to 14 minutes or until a wooden pick inserted in the center comes out almost clean.

▶ Meanwhile, stir together the strawberries, mango, and sugar substitute in a large bowl; toss gently yet thoroughly to blend. Let stand at room temperature while the cake is baking.

▶ Serve the cake warm or at room temperature with the fruit.

COOK'S NOTE: How do you tell if a mango is ripe? If it is dark in color, has a few spots on it, and "gives" when pressed lightly with the fingertips, it's ripe. To speed up the ripening process, place the mango in a paper bag 1 to 2 days at room temperature.

Excellent source of vitamin C

Banana Snack Squares with Pineapple and Coconut

Calories 150; total fat 4.5g (saturated fat 2g); protein 2g; carbohydrates 25g; fiber 1g; cholesterol 0mg; sodium 160mg; vitamin A 2%; vitamin C 4%; calcium 0%; iron 2%

1 6.4-ounce package banana muffin mix

½ cup water

1 8-ounce can crushed pineapple in juice, undrained

8 dried apricot halves, chopped

1 teaspoon cornstarch

½ cup sweetened flaked coconut

Makes 8 snack squares total

Serves 8 *(1 snack square per serving)*

▶ Preheat the oven to 375°F. Coat an 8-inch square nonstick baking pan with cooking spray.

▶ Combine the muffin mix and water in a medium bowl and stir until just moistened. Do not overmix. Spoon the batter into baking pan. (This will make a thin layer.) Bake 14 minutes or until the cake is a light golden brown and springs back when touched. Place cake on cooling rack and let stand 2 minutes before removing it from pan to cool slightly.

▶ Meanwhile, combine the remaining ingredients except the coconut in a small saucepan. Stir until the cornstarch is completely dissolved. Bring to a boil over high heat and boil 1 minute, stirring constantly. Remove from heat.

▶ Cut the cake into eight squares, spoon equal amounts of the pineapple mixture over each square, and sprinkle evenly with the coconut. Serve warm or at room temperature.

Gingerbread Rounds with Lemon Topping

Calories 150; total fat 4g (saturated fat 1g); protein 2g; carbohydrates 27g; fiber 1g; cholesterol 10mg; sodium 190mg; vitamin A 35%; vitamin C 2%; calcium 4%; iron 8%

Makes 16 rounds total

Serves 16 (*1 gingerbread round, 1 tablespoon whipped topping, and 1½ teaspoons pie filling per serving*)

1 14.5-ounce package gingerbread mix

½ 15-ounce can solid pumpkin

¼ cup egg substitute

1 cup water

1 cup fat-free whipped topping

½ cup lemon pie filling

▶ Preheat the oven to 350°F. Coat 16 nonstick muffin cups with cooking spray and set aside.

▶ Combine the gingerbread mix, pumpkin, egg substitute, and water in a medium bowl and mix according to the package directions.

▶ Spoon equal amounts of the batter into each muffin cup. Bake 10 minutes or until a wooden pick inserted in the center comes out clean. Place the tins on a cooling rack 5 minutes before removing the muffins.

▶ Serve warm or at room temperature with whipped topping and pie filling.

TIME-SHAVER TIP: What do you do with the remaining pumpkin? Place it in a small plastic bag and pop it into the freezer to have on hand for the next batch of rounds.

Excellent source of vitamin A

Chocolate Chip and Banana Pudding Cakes

Calories 150; total fat 4.5g (saturated fat 2g); protein 2g; carbohydrates 25g; fiber 1g; cholesterol 0mg; sodium 160mg; vitamin A 2%; vitamin C 4%; calcium 0%; iron 2%

Makes 8 cakes total

Serves 8 *(1 cake per serving)*

1 6.4-ounce package banana nut muffin mix

¼ cup mini semisweet chocolate chips

1 6-ounce jar pureed carrots (baby food)

⅓ cup water

½ teaspoon vanilla extract

½ cup wheat germ

1 tablespoon pourable sugar substitute, such as Splenda

¼ teaspoon ground cinnamon

▶ Preheat the oven to 425°F. Lightly spray eight 6-ounce ovenproof ramekins with cooking spray.

▶ In a medium bowl, combine the muffin mix, chocolate chips, carrots, water, and vanilla; stir until just moistened. Do not overmix.

▶ Spoon equal amounts of the batter into each ramekin, sprinkle evenly with the wheat germ, and bake 14 minutes or until the muffins are golden on top and a wooden pick inserted in the center comes out *almost* clean. Remove from the oven and let stand 5 minutes.

▶ Meanwhile, combine the sugar substitute with the cinnamon. Sprinkle evenly over all.

COOK'S NOTE: *This is a great recipe to keep on hand when warm comfort food is what you need.*

Blackberry Shortcakers

Calories 150; total fat 1.5g (saturated fat 0g); protein 3g; carbohydrates 31g; fiber 4g; cholesterol 0mg; sodium 270mg; vitamin A 2%; vitamin C 6%; calcium 6%; iron 8%

2 cups fresh, or frozen and thawed, blackberries

2½ tablespoons pourable sugar substitute, such as Splenda

½ teaspoon vanilla extract

¾ cup healthy pancake and baking mix, such as Bisquick Heart Smart

¼ cup fat-free milk

1 teaspoon grated orange rind

¼ cup whipped topping

> **Makes 4 shortcakes total**
>
> **Serves 4** *(1 shortcake, ½ cup berry mixture, and 1 tablespoon whipped topping per serving)*

▶ Preheat the oven to 425°F.

▶ Combine the berries, 1 tablespoon of the sugar substitute, and the vanilla in a medium bowl and toss gently yet thoroughly to blend. Set aside.

▶ Combine the baking mix, milk, remaining sugar substitute, and orange rind in a medium bowl; stir until just blended.

▶ Spoon batter onto a nonstick baking sheet in four mounds; bake 8 to 10 minutes or until golden on the *bottom*. Using a serrated knife, cut the mounds in half crosswise, and place the bottom halves in each of four dessert bowls or plates. Spoon equal amounts of the berries and any accumulated juices over each; top with whipped topping and the shortcake tops.

> **COOK'S NOTE:** *To create a sauce without any effort, cover the berry mixture and refrigerate overnight. It will release its juices, making a light sauce. The total yield of the berry mixture will be reduced from 2 cups to about 1 cup.*

Good source of fiber

Apricot Wheels

Calories 150; total fat 6g (saturated fat 1.5g); protein 3g; carbohydrates 21g; fiber 0g; cholesterol 0mg; sodium 310mg; vitamin A 4%; vitamin C 0%; calcium 0%; iron 6%

Serves 6 (2 wheels per serving)

9 dried apricot halves, chopped

3 tablespoons water

2 teaspoons grated orange rind

1 8-ounce package reduced-fat crescent dinner roll dough

Liquid butter spray, such as I Can't Believe It's Not Butter

2 teaspoons sugar

½ teaspoon ground cinnamon

▶ Preheat the oven to 375°F.

▶ Place the dried fruit, water, and orange rind in a microwave-safe bowl, cover with plastic wrap, and microwave on High for 1 minute. Stir and place on a dinner plate in a thin layer (along with any liquid) to cool quickly and allow the liquid to be absorbed; let stand 5 minutes, stirring frequently. (Note: Do not remove the dough from the refrigerator until the 5 minutes have passed.)

▶ On a clean work surface, unwrap and gently unroll the dough, keeping it in one piece—do not separate the dough. Spread the fruit mixture evenly over it. Starting on one of the long ends, roll up the dough, creating a long log. With seam side down and using a serrated knife, gently cut the dough into 12 slices, about ½ to ¾ inch each.

▶ Coat a nonstick baking sheet with cooking spray, place the dough "wheels" on the baking sheet, and bake 11 minutes or until golden. Spray each wheel with butter spray (1 spray per wheel); place the sugar and cinnamon in a fine sieve and sprinkle sugar mixture evenly over all. Serve immediately for peak flavor.

COOK'S NOTE: *When rolling up the dough to form a log, the seams may separate slightly. Tap them with your fingertips and they will seal easily. Don't handle the dough too much or it will become tough.*

Lemon-Orange Cream Bowls

Calories 150; total fat 0g (saturated fat 0g); protein 3g; carbohydrates 30g; fiber 0g; cholesterol 0mg; sodium 80mg; vitamin A 0%; vitamin C 25%; calcium 15%; iron 0%

3 cups fat-free whipped topping

2 6-ounce containers nonfat lemon yogurt sweetened with aspartame (1½ cups total)

¼ cup orange juice

¼ cup lemon juice

2 tablespoons pourable sugar substitute, such as Splenda

½ teaspoon lemon or vanilla extract

> **Makes about 4 cups cream total**
>
> **Serves 4** (*1 cup cream per serving*)

▶ Combine all ingredients in a medium bowl and stir until just blended. Spoon into four dessert bowls, parfait glasses, or wineglasses.

TIME-SAVER TIP: *Don't want to squeeze a lemon this time? Pick up the fresh but frozen variety in the supermarket, next to the orange juice concentrate.*

Excellent source of vitamin C

Good source of calcium

Tropical Fruit Custard Cups

Calories 150; total fat 2.5g (saturated fat 2g); protein 5g; carbohydrates 29g; fiber 2g; cholesterol 0mg; sodium 400mg; vitamin A 15%; vitamin C 50%; calcium 10%; iron 2%

1¾ cups fat-free milk

1 1-ounce package instant sugar-free, fat-free vanilla pudding mix

¼ teaspoon vanilla or coconut extract

1 ripe mango, peeled, seeded, and diced (about 1 cup)

1 cup chopped fresh pineapple

6 tablespoons sweetened flaked coconut

> **Makes 4 custard cups total**
>
> **Serves 4** *(½ cup custard, about ½ cup fruit, and 1 tablespoon coconut per serving)*

▶ Combine the milk, pudding mix, and extract in a medium bowl and whisk until smooth. Spoon equal amounts into each of four 6-ounce ramekins or wine goblets. Top with equal amounts of mango and pineapple, and sprinkle with coconut.

TIME-SHAVER TIP: Use a whisk rather than a spoon or fork to blend the mixture superfast.

Excellent source of vitamin C

Good source of vitamin A and calcium

Fresh Fruit in Rich Cinnamon Cream

Calories 150; total fat 0.5g (saturated fat 0g); protein 4g; carbohydrates 33g; fiber 5g; cholesterol 0mg; sodium 50mg; vitamin A 10%; vitamin C 190%; calcium 10%; iron 6%

1½ cups fat-free vanilla ice cream

½ teaspoon vanilla extract

½ teaspoon ground cinnamon

5 cups quartered strawberries

1 medium fresh peach or nectarine, sliced (1 cup)

Makes 6 cups fruit and about 1⅓ cups sauce total

Serves 4 (1½ cups fruit and about ⅓ cup sauce per serving)

▶ Combine the ice cream, vanilla, and cinnamon in a medium bowl; let stand for 15 minutes to soften slightly.

▶ Place equal amounts of the berries and peach slices in each of four shallow soup or dessert bowls. Stir the ice-cream mixture to a saucelike consistency and spoon evenly over each serving.

TIME-SHAVER TIP: This is the ultimate in easy. Anytime you need to whip up a sweet and creamy sauce in seconds for your family or friends, rely on this recipe—they'll never know! Spoon the sauce over the fruit or use it as a bed for the fruit to dress it up a bit.

Excellent source of fiber and vitamin C

Good source of vitamin A and calcium

Watermelon-Cranberry Splash

Calories 150; total fat 0g (saturated fat 0g); protein 2g; carbohydrates 27g; fiber 1g; cholesterol 0mg; sodium 5mg; vitamin A 25%; vitamin C 50%; calcium 2%; iron 4%

1 cup cranberry-raspberry or pomegranate juice

⅓ cup rum, vodka, or diet ginger ale

⅓ cup orange juice

1½ tablespoons lime juice

1½ tablespoons pourable sugar substitute, such as Splenda

1 teaspoon vanilla extract

6 cups watermelon cubes (about ¾ inch each)

Makes 6 cups watermelon cubes plus about 1¾ cups juice mixture total

Serves 4 *(1½ cups watermelon cubes and scant ½ cup juice mixture per serving)*

▶ Combine all ingredients, except the watermelon, in a small pitcher or a 2-cup measuring cup with a spout and stir until well blended. Spoon equal amounts of the watermelon into each of four large goblets or dessert bowls. Pour equal amounts of the juice mixture over each serving.

TIME-SHAVER TIP: *You can purchase precut melon in your supermarket's produce section, but you may need to cut the pieces a bit smaller. They need to be bite size to soak up the great flavors properly.*

Excellent source of vitamins A and C

Chai-Poached Pears and Blueberries

Calories 150; total fat 0g (saturated fat 0g); protein 1g; carbohydrates 41g; fiber 7g; cholesterol 0mg; sodium 0mg; vitamin A 2%; vitamin C 20%; calcium 2%; iron 2%

2 cups water

2 spiced chai teabags

2 tablespoons granulated sugar

4 firm medium pears, peeled, halved lengthwise, and cored (1½ pounds total)

2 teaspoons cornstarch

2 teaspoons grated lemon rind

1 cup fresh, or frozen and thawed, blueberries

> **Makes 8 pear halves plus ¾ cup sauce total**
>
> **Serves 4** *(2 pear halves, 3 tablespoons sauce, and ¼ cup blueberries per serving)*

▶ Bring all but 2 tablespoons of the water to a boil in a large nonstick skillet over medium-high heat. Remove from heat, add the teabags, and steep 3 minutes, moving the bags around frequently. Remove the teabags, squeezing excess liquid from the teabags into the skillet.

▶ Add the sugar and stir until dissolved. Add the pear halves, cut side down; bring to a boil over medium-high heat. Reduce heat, cover, and simmer 8 minutes or until just tender, turning occasionally. Place the pear halves on a rimmed platter or in a shallow pasta bowl.

▶ Combine the remaining 2 tablespoons water with the cornstarch and stir until completely dissolved; add the lemon rind and stir into the liquid in the skillet. Bring to a boil over medium-high heat and boil 1 minute, stirring frequently. Pour evenly over the pear halves and sprinkle berries on top. Serve hot, at room temperature, or chilled.

TIME-SHAVER TIP: Grated lemon rind may be stored in plastic wrap in the freezer to keep on hand for dishes like this one.

Excellent source of fiber and vitamin C

Hot Butterscotch Apples and Ice Cream

Calories 150; total fat 0g (saturated fat 0g); protein 3g; carbohydrates 37g; fiber 3g; cholesterol 0mg; sodium 85mg; vitamin A 6%; vitamin C 6%; calcium 8%; iron 2%

3 medium tart apples, such as Granny Smith, sliced (3 cups)

2 tablespoons raisins

2 tablespoons water

¼ teaspoon vanilla extract

3 tablespoons butterscotch or caramel ice-cream topping

1⅓ cups fat-free vanilla ice cream

Makes 2 cups apple mixture and 1⅓ cups ice cream total

Serves 4 *(⅓ cup ice cream and ½ cup apple mixture per serving)*

▶ Heat a large nonstick skillet over medium-high heat, and coat the skillet with cooking spray. Add the apples and raisins, coat them with cooking spray, and cook 8 minutes or until beginning to brown lightly, stirring frequently with two utensils as you would a stir-fry.

▶ Remove from heat, add the water and vanilla, and toss to blend. Drizzle the ice-cream topping evenly over all (do not stir), cover, and let stand 3 minutes to absorb flavor and soften slightly.

▶ Spoon equal amounts of the ice cream into each of four dessert bowls and top with equal amounts of the apple mixture.

COOK'S NOTE: Using a tart Granny Smith rather than a milder, sweeter apple variety gives a bit of contrast, boosting and defining the flavors instead of blending them.

Good source of fiber

Sour Cherry–Almond Pear Parfaits

Calories 150; total fat 2.5g (saturated fat 0g); protein 5g; carbohydrates 28g; fiber 3g; cholesterol 0mg; sodium 55mg; vitamin A 15%; vitamin C 10%; calcium 15%; iron 10%

1 14.5-ounce can sour pitted cherries in their own juice, undrained

1 large ripe pear, peeled, halved, cored, and diced (about 1¼ cups)

3 tablespoons pourable sugar substitute, such as Splenda

¼ teaspoon almond extract

2 6-ounce containers light vanilla yogurt (1½ cups total)

2 tablespoons sliced almonds, toasted and crushed

Makes 2½ cups cherry mixture, 1½ cups yogurt, and 2 tablespoons almonds total

Serves 4 (scant ⅔ cup cherry mixture, about ⅓ cup yogurt, and 1½ teaspoons almonds per serving)

▶ Combine the cherries and juice, pear, sugar substitute, and almond extract in a medium bowl; toss gently yet thoroughly to blend. Let stand 5 minutes to absorb flavors.

▶ To serve, place equal amounts in each of four parfait glasses or dishes, top with equal amounts of the yogurt, and sprinkle evenly with the almonds.

COOK'S NOTE: *Crushing the almonds helps distribute the rich flavor more evenly, giving an overall nutty flavor rather than a chunky texture to the dish.*

Good source of fiber, vitamins A and C, calcium, and iron

Appendix

Converting to Metrics

Volume Measurement Conversions

U.S.	Metric
¼ teaspoon	1.25ml
½ teaspoon	2.5ml
¾ teaspoon	3.75ml
1 teaspoon	5ml
1 tablespoon	15ml
¼ cup	62.5ml
½ cup	125ml
¾ cup	187.5ml
1 cup	250ml

Weight Measurement Conversions

U.S.	Metric
1 ounce	28.4g
8 ounces	227.5g
16 ounces (1 pound)	455g

Cooking Temperature Conversions

Celsius/Centigrade

0°C and 100°C are arbitrarily placed at the freezing and boiling points of water and are standard to the metric system.

Fahrenheit

0°F is the stabilized temperature when equal amounts of ice, water, and salt are mixed.

To convert temperatures in Fahrenheit to Celsius, use this formula:

$$C = (F - 32) \times 0.5555$$

So, for example, if a recipe calls for 350°F and you want to convert that temperature to Celsius, you would calculate it like this:

$$(350 - 32) \times 0.5555 = 176.65°C$$

Index

About the Author

Nancy S. Hughes is the author of ten nationally published cookbooks and has worked on more than thirty-five additional cookbooks for major organizations and corporations, such as Weight Watchers, *Cooking Light*, the American Heart Association, the American Diabetes Association, *Better Homes and Gardens*, Betty Crocker, and Publications International.

Her articles and recipes appear in national magazines, including *Favorite Brands*, *Diabetic Cooking*, *Cooking Pleasures*, and *Cooking Light*. She is also a consultant for food groups, such as the USA Rice Federation and Smart Balance.

She resides with her husband in Daphne, Alabama.